The Parent's Guide to In-Home ABA Programs

of related interest

Understanding Applied Behavior Analysis
An Introduction to ABA for Parents, Teachers, and other Professionals
Albert J. Kearney
ISBN 978 1 84310 860 3
eISBN 978 1 84642 726 8
Part of the JKP Essentials series

Applied Behaviour Analysis and Autism
Building A Future Together
Edited by Mickey Keenan, Mary Henderson, Ken P. Kerr and Karola Dillenburger
Foreword by Professor Gina Green
ISBN 978 1 84310 310 3
eISBN 978 1 84642 455 7

The Verbal Behavior Approach
How to Teach Children with Autism and Related Disorders
Mary Lynch Barbera with Tracy Rasmussen
Foreword by Mark L. Sundberg, Ph.D., BCBA
ISBN 978 1 84310 852 8
eISBN 978 1 84642 653 7

A Step-by-Step Curriculum for Early Learners
with Autism Spectrum Disorders
Lindsay Hilsen MEd, BCBA
ISBN 978 1 84905 874 2

A Brief Guide to Autism Treatments
Elisabeth Hollister Sandberg and Becky L. Spritz
ISBN 978 1 84905 904 6
eISBN 978 0 85700 650 9

Video Modeling for Young Children with
Autism Spectrum Disorders
A Practical Guide for Parents and Professionals
Sarah Murray and Brenna Noland
ISBN 978 1 84905 900 8
eISBN 978 0 85700 638 7

THE PARENT'S GUIDE TO

In-Home

ABA

Programs

Frequently Asked Questions about Applied
Behavior Analysis for your Child with Autism

ELLE OLIVIA JOHNSON

Jessica Kingsley *Publishers*
London and Philadelphia

The photographs of children have been printed with kind permission from their parents.

First published in 2013
by Jessica Kingsley Publishers
116 Pentonville Road
London N1 9JB, UK
and
400 Market Street, Suite 400
Philadelphia, PA 19106, USA

www.jkp.com

Library of Congress Cataloging in Publication Data
A CIP catalog record for this book is available from the Library of Congress

British Library Cataloguing in Publication Data
A CIP catalogue record for this book is available from the British Library

ISBN 978 1 84905 918 3
eISBN 978 0 85700 725 4

Printed and bound in the United States

Contents

Chapter 2 During the Session. 39

Part 2: Programming, Lingo, and Data Collection

Part 3: Getting More Involved and Looking to the Future

Acknowledgements

To my beloved wife, Jeanette, and our amazing son, Miles, I love you both more than you can ever imagine. You make every day brighter and more meaningful, and I am so happy to call you my family.

To Sue French, Rachel Page, Mia Healy, Heather Samokhvalof, Kim and Jenna Sleichter, Christie and Trevor Dougherty, and Katie Johnson, I count you among my closest friends and am honored that you have included me in your lives.

To my editor, Emily McClave, thank you for your guidance and support on this project. Your leadership helped bring this book to completion, and I am very grateful.

To the many families I have worked with, both in the home and in the classroom, thank you for granting me the honor and the privilege of teaching your children.

Introduction

The number of children diagnosed with, or considered at-risk for autism has dramatically increased and now 1 in every 88 children has been identified with an autism spectrum disorder, according to the Centers for Disease Control (CDC, 2012). One of the best and most effective ways to treat autism's behaviors and educational deficits is through early treatment with applied behavior analysis, or ABA. However, many parents who are faced with the very real possibility that their child has a disability have many questions: What is ABA? How can ABA be used to help my child? What is my role as a parent? How can I help?

This book will answer your questions! Written in easy-to-understand language, it will take you through the basics of ABA, describe what a typical ABA program looks like, and help you understand the lingo that the ABA team uses. It is written in a simple question-and-answer format that makes it easy to find exactly what you are looking for. You will learn the very least you need to know, and will receive information on how to take your understanding and practical usage of ABA much further.

When I began working with young children considered at-risk for autism, I quickly realized that many, many,

many families asked me the same questions. Usually, those questions focused on their child and the ABA program, but many questions dealt with our relationship as a therapist and family, on my opinions regarding the outcome they should expect, and on various aspects of the data we collect. You will find answers to all these questions here, from how to read and understand the data collected by your child's ABA therapist, to the propriety of including your ABA therapist in your social life.

Each chapter begins with a vignette that serves as an example of a situation that many families who have children with autism face. None of these examples are real-life stories; however, they are all based in real situations I have observed during my time working with children on the autism spectrum. You may see similarities between these examples and your own life, but remember, each child with autism is different and each child with autism will have a different story. What works for one child and family may not work for another.

Note: For ease of reading, the male pronoun has been used throughout the book when referring to a single unspecified person.

PART I

The Basics of ABA Home Programming

CHAPTER 1

Getting Started

Vignette: Mia and Robbie

• •

Mia is a 23-year-old single mother of three children, Robbie, Benny, and Joseph. Joseph and Benny are four-year-old twins, and Robbie is two and a half. Benny and Joseph seem to be doing well, but Robbie has been exhibiting severe behavior problems since his second birthday. He refuses to eat anything other than pretzels and yogurt, insists on drinking only out of his favorite bottle, and tantrums when his mother tries to put his shoes on. He repeatedly fills up and dumps out bins of toys and drops heavy objects on the tile floors. He is so loud, in fact, that Mia's landlord has told her that neighbors have complained about his crying and loud bangs coming from their apartment. Mia worries that she will be evicted and cannot imagine how her life could be any more difficult. What's more, Robbie has become almost silent and rarely plays with his brothers. He usually chooses the same toy, takes it to the corner, and plays alone.

Mia's friend, Jenna, told her that Robbie might be able to be helped by a doctor. Mia takes Robbie to her local clinic, where the doctor suspects autism. Over the next two months, Robbie is given a provisional diagnosis of autism and assigned to an in-home ABA (applied behavior analysis) agency. The agency will be coming for their first visit on Monday. Mia worries that they will think that she has not been a good parent, and is confused about what ABA really is. She has never even heard of it! Is it going to help her son? How can she help? What should she expect?

As a parent new to ABA in-home programming, Mia has many questions. What is ABA? How is it used? How might it affect Robbie's future? What will my role be?

. . . .

1. What is ABA?

ABA stands for applied behavior analysis: a scientific approach to evaluating and changing behavior that is backed by years of research and analysis. ABA focuses on improving behaviors of social significance to a meaningful degree; it is rooted in the principles of behavior such as positive reinforcement and extinction, and systematically utilizes behavior change tactics derived from those principles; it targets behaviors that are observable and measurable, and is driven by data; and, it is generalizable, striving to have outcomes that last over time.

Whew! That's a lot to take in! Let's delve a little further into what ABA really is. Don't worry; we'll take a look at some examples to make things even more clear. To start, we will look at the first part of that definition.

Behaviors targeted for change are socially significant and the intent is to improve the quality of life for that individual and those involved in his life. For example, a three-year-old child with autism who is spending hours running circles in the living room is obviously exhibiting a behavior that needs to be altered in some way. When he begins to attend preschool, it is not in his best interests to run in circles at school, unable to settle down and learn. This behavior is viewed by ABA as a socially significant one... that is, if this child was running in circles for roughly two minutes a day, that behavior would be seen as less serious and less in need of change. A three-year-old child who is spending hours running in circles is exhibiting a behavior that is seriously impeding his social skills, communication, and learning. Significantly improving this behavior would increase this child's quality of life as well as the quality of life of those around him.

Because ABA doesn't just deal with problem behavior, it might help to look at another aspect of socially significant behavior. The first example looked at how ABA was used to *decrease* a socially significant behavior, now, let's look at how ABA can be used to *increase* a socially significant behavior. Imagine Trevor, a ten-year-old boy with autism. He has a sister, Kim, who is eight. Kim earns an allowance by caring for the family's guinea pig and goldfish. Trevor's parents would like him to also earn an allowance by completing a daily chore. The family, classroom teacher, and in-home supervisor meet as a team to discuss how the responsibility of a chore at home can effectively tie in to Trevor's educational and self-care goals. The team decides to teach Trevor to set the table for dinner every night. When an alarm clock rings at 4:45, Trevor will go to the kitchen, retrieve the needed plates, utensils, cups, and napkins, and will independently set the table.

At first, Trevor seemed to be doing well with his chore. He gathered the correct amount of dinnerware and placed them in the correct place on the table. On closer inspection, however, Trevor's parents noticed that he almost always placed the four knives at one place setting, four spoons at another, and four forks at a third. The fourth place setting received no utensils at all!

Trevor's in-home program supervisor designed an intervention to address the problem. The first week, Trevor practiced setting just one place setting correctly, using a photo of a correctly set table as a reference. His father shadowed him, pointing out mistakes immediately so that Trevor could correct them. Once he achieved this goal, he received a small increase in his allowance. The second week, Trevor learned to set two place settings correctly. Again, he received a small increase in his allowance. The plan continued until Trevor could set all four place settings independently. The photo was gradually used less often until Trevor stopped needing it. Trevor was proud of his "raises" and his family was proud of his success and contributions to the family!

ABA practitioners use the principles of behavior such as positive reinforcement, extinction, self-management, positive behavior supports, as well as many techniques based on those principles to change behavior. By looking closely at the program the ABA program supervisor developed, we can see how specific steps helped Trevor learn this new skill: The photo served as an easy reference for Trevor to follow while learning his task (a visual prompt), the alarm clock gave him a clearly defined schedule of when to begin setting the table (an audible prompt), and Trevor's father acting as a shadow gave Trevor the opportunity to learn the task correctly.

Back to that definition of ABA. Behaviors targeted are measurable and observable, with a strong emphasis on data. Practitioners rely heavily on data to make decisions regarding program progress and change. You might find that your ABA therapist takes data on everything from the response to the words, "Come sit," to the way in which they touch putty, to whether or not they wave goodbye. More about data and data collection later.

Finally…ABA programming will plan for generalization so that behavior changes will be long lasting. Practitioners will teach children to generalize skills across various settings and situations, with various people and materials, during different times of day, and even to other behaviors. In the future, Trevor might have a job where he needs to assemble or prepare items, or where he needs to begin or complete a task by a certain time. His practical experience at home gives him valuable skills and shows that Trevor can be taught a difficult task with some simple supports.

2. Why is ABA being used with my child?

ABA is widely considered to be one of the best ways to treat children and adults with autism. It gives teachers, ABA therapists, parents, and everyone else involved with a child with autism the tools they need to change behavior. You can view ABA as a toolbox: it contains various techniques that, when used correctly, can change socially significant behavior. The ABA practitioner will take detailed data on a problem behavior, analyze that data, and then use the ABA "toolbox" to select the most appropriate technique that can be used to alter the problem behavior. You wouldn't call a TV repairman to fix the washing machine, would you? The same practical rules ring true for ABA therapy: if you have a child with autism, who has problem behavior, ABA therapy is a respected, research-driven, effective way to treat children with autism.

3. At what age should my child start an ABA program?

The sooner, the better! If you feel that your child might possibly benefit from ABA services, or suspect that your child has autism or another developmental disability, obtain help as soon as possible by having them professionally assessed by their pediatrician or other qualified medical professional. The sooner you obtain early intervention services for your child, and the sooner you learn the techniques and methods used by ABA practitioners and educators, the sooner you will begin to see results with your child.

4. What can I expect when my ABA program begins?

You may first have a meeting at the agency's office or at your home. This will be a time when you can ask questions, fill out forms, and learn who will be on the team that will be working with your child. Present may be the agency director, team supervisor, behavioral therapists, or other service providers involved in the case, such as an occupational therapist or physical therapist. During this initial meeting, the ABA agency will discuss with you your child's needs, and the needs of you and your family. They will also make a plan to begin assessing your child. These assessments may be done through interviews, standardized assessments, observations of home or school environments, and actual interaction with your child and the ABA supervisor and therapists. If you have specific concerns about your child or concerns about their academic, self-help, or communication needs, the assessment period is a great time to discuss these concerns. The ABA team will work with you to determine if these skills need to be immediately addressed and added to a program of intervention, or if they are age-appropriate for typically developing children.

Next, the ABA team will begin to assess your child. When the ABA team conducts an informal assessment of your child's skills, it may appear that they are doing little more than playing. The therapist, however, is using this time to develop a rapport with your child while also assessing their abilities. The therapist wants your child to see them as a fun buddy who comes to the house a few times a week to play, not as a strict disciplinarian who demands that your child stack unending towers of blocks. For this reason, the therapist will use tasks interspersed with play to motivate and teach your child. Many times, the therapist is probing behavior and ability, that is, is gently testing your child to see what skills they have, and what skills may need to be worked on. The ABA team will spend a week or two evaluating your child in this way, before deciding on particular goals to work on.

5. How much time will it take?

ABA sessions may take between one and three hours, with occasional sessions lasting longer (particularly if the session involves a social outing, to the grocery store, for example). The number of sessions your child receives per week will depend on several factors such as the needs of your child, available funding, and approval from the funding source. Some children will receive just a few hours of ABA therapy per week while others will receive over 20 hours per week. Generally, ABA programs start with two or three days a week, and that time may be increased as the child becomes more accustomed to the format and demands of the instruction. It's important to realize that even if your child begins with just a few hours a week, the ABA therapist will give you specific things to practice with your child. It is essential that you help your child practice the skills they are learning in their ABA sessions in all areas of his life.

6. What if I don't like my child's therapist?

The world is made up of many different people with many different personalities. We're bound to encounter someone sooner or later that we just don't *get*. However, even if you don't *get* the therapist that is coming to your home, give them a chance. The program supervisor and agency has already taken into consideration the personality of your child, the therapist, and YOU. A firm therapist with a great sense of humor might be an excellent fit with your serious child, or a mellow therapist with a no-nonsense style might be just the ticket to work with a child who has some severe behaviors. Let it play out and you will probably be thrilled with the match.

7. What if my child doesn't like the therapist?

Here is how the first month of sessions may go: The ABA therapist builds rapport with your child for two weeks. Everything is going great! Your child runs to the door when he hears that Katie is here, or even sits at his little table when she sees Bob walk in the room. But once the ABA therapist begins to make demands on your child, the honeymoon period might be over. Your child might cry or tantrum when the ABA therapist asks them to do difficult tasks. Don't worry! The ABA therapist is an expert on changing behavior, and if they see that your child isn't having a good time, they will change their approach. This isn't to say that children should *never* cry during sessions. They might cry. They might cry for the entire two hours, and it's important to remember that it's OK! If you were to use a timer and track the amount of time your child cries during session, you would probably see that the amount of time they cry varies over time, but ultimately decreases in the long run. The therapist is pushing your child beyond their comfort zone in an effort to help him learn new skills, which can be difficult at times, but stick with it. Consistency will help your child progress!

8. My ABA therapist is "in training." Can't I have a therapist who is more experienced?

Sometimes, an ABA therapist may move from one agency to another. Although much of the programming used in agencies is similar, there may be differences in data collection, reinforcement, or verbal instructions. A new hire to any ABA agency will undergo a period of "training," where they become familiar with the techniques and paperwork used by their new agency. Having a therapist who is "in training" may not necessarily indicate a lack of experience; rather, it may be more indicative of a therapist's need to familiarize themselves with their new employer. If, after several weeks, you feel like the therapist is not familiar with the programming, or there are other concerns, by all means speak with the program supervisor.

9. What qualifications should an ABA therapist have? Can I ask them about their background and special interests?

Agency qualifications vary. Many ABA agencies require their therapists to have at least a Bachelor's degree, while others will hire a promising employee who has some college credit and experience with special needs children. Even better, many agencies are now requiring that therapists complete coursework and supervision as specified by the Behavior Analyst Certification Board®, or BACB®. The BACB® is an international organization dedicated to the education, ethical and legal standards, certification, and continuing education of behavior analysts in three categories:

- Board Certified Behavior Analyst (BCBA®): Certificant holds at least a Master's degree.

- Board Certified Assistant Behavior Analysts (BCaBA®): Certificant holds at least a Bachelor's degree.

- Board Certified Behavior Analyst—Doctoral (BCBA-D®): Certificant has completed a doctoral program of study, and has already been certified as a BCBA®.

The BACB® certifies those who have completed extensive, BACB®-approved ABA coursework. The coursework, supervision requirements, and certification exam are rigorous and extensive. You can find much more information about behavior analyst certification at the BACB's® website, www.bacb.com, including information for consumers and a certificant registry.

Definitely ask your ABA therapist about their background and interests! It might be surprising to you to learn that your ABA therapist has an advanced degree or a personal interest that matches your own. Even within the field of autism, there are specific interests and specializations: feeding disorders, school-aged children with autism, Asperger's syndrome etc. You'll probably be pleased to learn that the therapist is not only an autism professional, but is also deeply involved in the autism "community" as well.

10. Why doesn't my ABA therapist know anything about biomedical treatments?

ABA is a research-based, data-driven science. All techniques used in ABA have been thoroughly reviewed by ABA professionals and have been proven through research. Your ABA therapist should not recommend any intervention that is not peer-reviewed and research-based. Their training, education, and experience are in ABA, and non-ABA techniques, such as biomedical interventions, are not considered part of ABA. Many, many parents have questions regarding biomedical interventions such as vitamin shots, gluten-free diets, dairy-free diets, and chelation. These interventions are not considered to be part of ABA. If you are interested in trying a biomedical intervention, look for peer-reviewed research. Review the study carefully, paying special attention to the number of subjects in the study, who provided funding for the study, and the year the study was published. Learning to read research articles with a critical eye is another of your responsibilities as an advocate for your child.

11. The program supervisor told me that two different therapists would be coming to see my child. Wouldn't it be easier to have just one person?

Usually, early intervention programs require that more than one therapist see a child. The reason for this is that in order to move a child forward through a program (increasing the difficulty of a program as a child makes progress, for example), the child needs to show mastery of a task with at least two therapists. The reason for this is that, for example, although little Annie can match colors with her beloved therapist Daniel, she seems unsure when asked to do so by other people. The requirement of mastery with at least two therapists gives the ABA program supervisor valuable information about the child's level of understanding and generalization. Every behavioral therapist has a slightly different style, and program changes cannot be made until it is determined that the child can show mastery of the task with at least two instructors. Different ABA programs may require different degrees of mastery, but it is usually 80–90 percent success rate on three consecutive sessions, using a variety of materials, and with at least two therapists.

12. What does a supervisor do?

The supervisor for your child's ABA program has a variety of responsibilities. They develop goals for your child and monitor the subsequent programs for success. They are responsible for training and supervising the staff that works with your child, and for writing reports that detail your child's progress. Most program changes come about through supervisor evaluation, and although the therapists may move your child forward through their program, the supervisor will oversee any significant changes. They should provide you with information about autism and any other disabilities your child has been diagnosed with. When your child transitions from their in-home ABA program to preschool, the supervisor will work closely with the school or district to plan and help carry out the necessary assessments and meetings.

As a participant in an early childhood education program, your child may have either an IEP (Individualized Education Plan) or an IFSP (Individualized Family Service Plan). In the United States, in most states, the IFSP is a plan that stays in place from birth through age two, and concentrates on helping your child reach developmental milestones. The IEP has a more academic focus and is intended to assist your child in reaching education milestones. The supervisor should be able to answer the questions you might have regarding the IEP process, and should know where to refer you if you have questions they cannot answer.

13. What does that ABA agency do?

An ABA agency is responsible for developing and implementing the ABA program that will be used to teach your child. The agency will assign a case supervisor, who will develop programs for your child, train staff, and report on your child's progress. In many cases, the ABA agency provides all toys and materials used in sessions. The ABA agency also will plan and hold clinic meetings, where your child and their progress will be discussed with every member of the team. These meetings may take place in the home or agency office.

The ABA agency assists with the IEP process and the transition of your child into preschool or kindergarten. Some ABA agencies serve children up to age three, and others serve children past the age of three. If you are fortunate to have service past the age of three, the goals of the program will change from pre-academic skills to functional living skills, such as dressing, feeding, and independent work. The school system will be responsible for the academic skills at this point.

ABA agencies may hire therapists as either employees or consultants. Employees earn sick time, vacation time, and enjoy other benefits such as agency-planned schedules and insurance. Consultants typically make more money per hour, but are responsible for their expenses such as insurance, business cards, toys and office supplies. Consultants also typically have more freedom over their own schedules and locations they are willing to work.

14. What is a mandated reporter?

A mandated reporter is a person who is legally obligated to report suspected child abuse or neglect. A mandated reporter is compelled by the law to report incidents of suspected abuse or neglect. Don't worry if your child falls and hits his head on the coffee table. It is very unlikely that the ABA therapist will find it necessary to see this as a case that meets the requirements for reporting. They *will* probably document the injury or bruise in their notes, both for your protection and theirs. Be assured that agencies take VERY seriously their role as mandated reporters, and that reports of abuse and neglect are not made without serious consideration and discussion.

Examples of mandated reporters are:

- doctors

- nurses

- teachers and school personnel

- ABA therapists

- speech therapists

- occupational therapists

- physical therapists

- police officers

- anyone else who works with children in a professional capacity.

15. What if I see a disconnect between ABA therapy and speech therapy, occupational therapy, etc?

Practitioners of ABA understand that by reinforcing or NOT reinforcing a behavior, we can affect how that behavior occurs in the future. It is not uncommon to find speech pathologists, occupational therapists, or other service providers who have no training in ABA, or who have not had the opportunity to work with a child who is also receiving ABA therapy. This is why it is so important to collaborate as a team! Parents, ABA providers, and all the other service providers who work with a child should "be on the same page." Sometimes, all it takes is a meeting with everyone on the team, where each practitioner has an opportunity to discuss how to best serve the child. If you have concerns that your child's service providers are not "on the same page," you may wish to discuss having a meeting where everyone can come together and participate in a whole-team approach.

16. Is ABA the same as discrete trial training?

Good question! ABA is the study of and application of techniques used for behavior change. Discrete trial training (DTT) is just one of those techniques that ABA therapists use to change behavior. Remember that ABA "toolbox"? Well, DTT is one of the many tools that ABA practitioners use.

But wait, just what IS DTT? It is a one-to-one teaching method that maximizes learning by breaking skills into small components that can be taught *discretely*, that is, with a clear beginning and end. The therapist's instruction (the antecedant) is followed by a response (the behavior), and elicits a consequence (the reward, or reinforcer, or the non-presentation of a reward or reinforcer). DTT is an excellent tool for ABA therapists because it allows for multiple opportunities to respond within a short period of time, and thus allows for multiple opportunities for the therapist to reinforce (or not) the behavior that occurs. ABA therapists will use praise and tangible reinforcers to increase the likelihood that the response to their instruction will occur the same way in the future. Finally, ABA therapists take detailed data when conducting a DTT session, and calculate the percentage of correct responses at the end of the session, as this data is vital when assessing a child's progress.

Below is an example of a DTT instructional session:

Therapist (sitting across from two-year-old Lucy, at a small table): "Clap your hands."

Lucy claps her hands.

Therapist: "Yay! Good job." (*Records data.*)

Therapist: "Lucy, touch your nose."

Lucy taps the top of her head.

Therapist: "Mmm, let's try again. Touch your nose." (*This time the therapist gently guides Lucy's hand to touch the tip of her nose.*)

Therapist: "OK, you did it!"

Therapist: "Touch your nose."

Lucy touches her nose independently.

Therapist: "Hooray! You are so smart! Let's blow some bubbles!"

The example on the previous page shows how the therapist gives Lucy the opportunity to respond independently, assists her with her response, and the reaction to her correct response. DTT sessions include many opportunities for response, and the therapist will prompt your child as necessary. DTT is often the first step in many in-home programs. As your child gains skills that generalize to a variety of environments, DTT is often gradually faded out and instruction is conducted in a more natural, less "teachy" manner.

17. I've heard that ABA, and especially DTT, will make my child robotic. Is that true?

No! If you sit and watch a DTT session closely, however, you will see how an experienced therapist easily works drills and reinforcement into the session, in a way that your child may not even realize. Watch carefully, and you will see how the therapist easily intersperses tasks into play. Children who are able to handle more repetition may have tasks that require them to attend for longer periods of time. The ABA therapist, just like an actor in a play, can present and re-present the same material repeatedly, but each time it seems like new.

18. I'm uncomfortable with strangers in my home. Can't we do sessions at the agency's office instead?

While it would sometimes be convenient to have ABA sessions done at an office or school, it is vitally important that most ABA therapy be done at home, in the child's natural environment. Not only will your child be learning in an environment where they are most comfortable, but also you as the parent will be able to directly participate in sessions. Even if your child receives ABA therapy for three hours, five days a week, YOU are their primary influence for the remaining 21 hours a day. You need to learn how to implement all the behavioral techniques that the therapist is using with your child. It's as if your child was learning a new language... you wouldn't expect to send your child to a language class and have them come home speaking a new language, and expect to understand it. ABA techniques are their new language, and it's important that you learn to "speak" this language as well.

19. I have to work. Can sessions be done at daycare every day?

Generally not. ABA programs require that parents be closely involved, and if a session is completed at daycare every day, parents don't have the opportunity to learn. In fact, some state agencies may have restrictions on the amount of time ABA services can be provided outside of the home environment. Talk to the program supervisor, and see if it's possible for the program to include one or two days a week at daycare. If it's allowed by the state agency funding the program, it may be a possibility. Also keep in mind that the therapist may work in a specific region of your city, and if the daycare program is significantly far from your home, they may not be able to accommodate your request.

20. What are my responsibilities as a parent?

As a parent, you are responsible for a lot!

- Your child should be ready to learn at the start of session. This includes being clean and dressed before the ABA therapist enters your home. If your child naps before session, make sure that they have at least 30 minutes to wake up fully before session begins.

- Try not to pack too many things into your schedule. Remember, your child needs time to breathe and relax between educational sessions. If they have speech therapy in the morning, occupational therapy at noon, and ABA at 3:30, they are basically working like a full-time adult. Don't forget to include some simple playtime too.

- If you think that your child will be hungry, please give them a snack before session begins.

- If you think that your child might need a snack during session, ask the therapist when would be a good time to do so. Popping in with chips when your child is being asked to complete a task will interrupt session and possibly reinforce the wrong behavior.

- You must be available during session to assist the behavioral consultant. This might include changing a dirty diaper, wiping a yucky nose, or finding a snack for the child.

- You are responsible for ensuring that the location for therapy remains consistently quiet. If older siblings returning from school like to use the playroom for video games in the afternoons, then an ABA session held there won't work.

- Cancel session if your child is sick. This is probably the number one request of ABA therapists! If your child has a fever, diarrhea, or a terribly runny nose within 24 hours prior to their ABA session, you need to cancel. Therapists see as many as three children a day, up to 18 children a week (and the supervisor sometimes many more!), so one sick child can easily spread illness to everyone else on that therapist's caseload.

- Remember the 50/50 rule. The therapist is only responsible for 50 percent of the program. The other 50 percent of the responsibility for the success of your child's ABA program lies with you. This means that you must learn about ABA, master the programs and techniques used by the therapist, and learn how to implement them without the therapist's presence. This also means asking questions, reading material provided by the ABA program, doing your own research, and helping other family members understand that the ABA program can significantly impact your child's life for the better. It's a big challenge, but one that you will be able to accomplish with the help of the ABA team.

- Last but not least, you are responsible for implementing the ABA program in the absence of the therapist. A good ABA program will train you to implement the techniques used by the therapists in every aspect of your child's life.

21. What is "parent training"?

Parent training is an umbrella term that covers all the information your child's team tailors to *your* needs. The agency that serves your child may have specific parent training topics they will provide information on, such as general autism information or basic behavioral change training. They can also provide parent training on any topic that they decide might benefit your child and your family. Many state agencies require a certain amount of time be spent on parent training, and some agencies require that you receive a certain amount of parent training even before sessions can begin in your home. Think of parent training as an opportunity to learn tools and techniques that will stay in your ABA "toolbox" for life.

CHAPTER 2

During the Session

Vignette: Rachel and Peter

Rachel has just begun working with two-year-old Peter. As she walks up the steps to Peter's home, she mentally reviews some of his communication goals: eye contact, vocalizations, and pretend play skills. She rings the bell and is excited to see Peter has accompanied his mother to the door. Rachel waves, says "Hi Peter!" and crouches down to his level. As soon as Peter glances her way, she pulls out a toy train from her bag and lets Peter play with it for a minute or two. Peter then lets her gently lead him from the foyer to the table set up in the living room. As Peter's mother settles down on the sofa to watch, Rachel turns to Peter and says, "Can I have a turn?", at the same time putting her hand out, palm up. Peter places the train in her palm and excitedly waits for Rachel to open the bin of toys. As Peter plays with a few toys that Rachel has set out, Rachel reviews his binder and makes a plan for today's session.

First, Rachel works on a compliance goal with Peter. She calls out, "Come sit," and Peter reluctantly leaves his toys on the floor. Rachel praises him as he sits down in his chair. She pulls out one of Peter's favorite trains from her pocket, and Peter's face immediately changes from one of disappointment to one of elation. Rachel jots down a few notes and places a wooden puzzle on the table. She asks Peter for the train, and he seems to pretend that he doesn't hear her. Rachel asks again, this time with her hand out, and Peter places the train in her hand. Rachel has already removed the puzzle pieces from the puzzle, and says to Peter, "Finish the puzzle." As soon as Peter completes the puzzle, Rachel gives him his preferred train back. The rest of the session proceeds in much the same way: work tasks that target specific goals, interspersed with lots of play and fun time. At the end of the two-hour session, Rachel has worked on almost all of Peter's goals. He hasn't even realized that he's been working! To Peter, the two-hour session was just a fun time playing with his buddy.

• •

I. Where in the house should we do the session?

ABA therapy sessions can be done almost anywhere. I have provided therapy services in a kitchen, garage, front lawn, bedroom, living room, even a walk-in closet. The criteria for an ideal place to do a session are simple: It needs to be clean, comfortable, and relatively free of distractions.

And remember, things that don't bother you and me may be very distracting for a child with autism. The program supervisor or therapist can offer suggestions for a location if you aren't sure. Beautiful wooden or tile floors can be torturous for a therapist who is sitting on the ground for the majority of session. A carpeted room or even a comfy floor pillow is very much appreciated!

Vignette: Tommy

Tommy has just begun receiving services for autism. During his first ABA session, the therapist was pleased to see that Tommy would be doing session in the living room, which was clean, had beautiful hardwood floors with a luxurious rug, and quiet. However, the therapist noticed almost immediately that Tommy was extremely distracted by the glare from the television. He also wanted to run his fingers through the fringe on the rug, and he tried to every chance he could get. When a blanket covered the TV, Tommy tried to catch his reflection in framed photos on the wall, glossy photos in a book…anything! A simple location change to a carpeted area of the playroom solved the problem…Tommy was quickly back on track and engaged in his program.

2. What does a typical ABA session involve?

An expert ABA therapist can work on a multitude of goals while your child thinks they are playing. Depending on your child's individual needs and program, the ABA therapist may work on goals that target communication, problem solving, compliance (such as following directions), or play skills (such as taking turns during a game or engaging in pretend play with the therapist). The session will also usually include at least one 10–15 minute break, during which your child will have the opportunity to have a snack, diaper change if necessary, and the therapist will have a chance to catch up on notes and plan for the second half of the session.

You will probably be directly involved in the session at least once per hour. Your involvement may involve taking data, actively teaching your child, or sometimes just being in the room as a distractor. Finally, the beginning or end of the session includes time for the therapist to complete paperwork and notes. You may also find the beginning or end of a session a good time to ask specific questions regarding your child's behavior. If you think that your questions may take more than 5 or 10 minutes, let your therapist know so that they can end a few minutes early to accommodate you.

3. How can I participate in sessions?

There are a myriad of ways to participate in the ABA session. Initially, the ABA therapist might ask that you watch quietly from the same room. Once you have a feel for the format of the session, you might be trained to take data or directly teach your child. At the very least, you should be available to assist the therapist if they have questions or need materials. Sometimes, the presence of a parent in the room is very distracting for a child. Your first job as a parent learning the ins and outs of an ABA program may be to simply sit on the sofa, watching the program and learning to not jump in when your child is having difficulty! You would be surprised to learn just how many children try to leave the instructional area to be "saved" by mom or dad when things get difficult! Almost every in-home client I have had has needed a few weeks of mom or dad's presence as observers!

4. Can my child have an ABA session while I take a nap, watch a movie, or go shopping?

No. ABA agencies require that parents be actively involved in the session. This might include taking data, learning behavioral intervention techniques, running programs and giving directions, etc. You need to remain available to be involved in session. You might get lucky and have a chance to throw a load of laundry in or wash the dishes, but don't count on it. Session is for BOTH the family and the child.

5. I have an appointment and must end the session early or cancel it. Is that OK?

Sure! Therapists understand that life sometimes interrupts, and it may be necessary to shorten or cancel a session. Remember a few things, though…

- Some ABA therapists work full time, and may only be in your region for two or three days per week. Ending a session early might leave your therapist with some extra time to fill, so be polite and let them know at least 24 hours in advance. This will give the therapist time to adjust their schedule and/ or drive time for appointments. Calling the therapist ten minutes before the appointment is to begin is not acceptable.

- If you frequently have to cancel an appointment due to arriving late from work or another scheduling conflict, it would be greatly appreciated by the agency and the therapist if you would consider permanently changing the time to one that works better for you.

- Never cancel by email less than 48 hours before the session is to begin. If you don't receive a confirmation email within 24 hours in return, call the office.

6. My ABA therapist had to cancel a session, and has offered to make it up. How does this work?

ABA therapists, whether they are attached to an agency or working as an independent contractor, are equally concerned that your child receive as much ABA therapy as possible. If, for example, your child has been awarded ten hours of ABA per week, that ABA therapist wants to be sure that your child receives that amount. If illness or personal emergency necessitates a cancellation, your child's therapist *may* be able to reschedule that session. Their ability to make up the session depends on several things: your availability, their availability, and the possibility that a substitute may be able to cover the session. If a substitute is available to see your child instead of the regular ABA therapist, the agency will let you know ASAP.

7. My child's therapist brings her own toys. Are these clean?

Some agencies hire ABA therapists as independent contractors. Independent contractors are responsible for purchasing, maintaining, and cleaning their own toys. However, another client might not have necessarily used that bag of toys that day. Some independent contractors have a bag for each child they see, and toys never mix. If you have a concern about the cleanliness of toys, ask the therapist if the toys are dedicated to your child, and if not, to wipe them down with an antibacterial wipe before session begins. The therapist will always remove and clean a toy that has been with an ill child before using it again. Additionally, they will frequently inspect toys for wear and safety.

8. I really want my child to be able to say his name. Why aren't we working on it?

Your child may not have the prerequisite skills needed to say his or her name, and one of the programs already in place may be teaching those skills. To answer the question, "What is your name?" your child needs to be able to attend to the questioner, process the question, know the answer, and must have the speech capability to answer. The ABA therapist can tell you more about the specific steps your child is working on.

9. Can my child's siblings play in the session too?

This is a question that is asked very frequently, and it has a simple answer. If your child can benefit from having a sibling in the session, it *may* be possible for them to join the session for a brief period. A "brief time" might be the last 15 minutes at the end of session, which may be used as an opportunity for your child to practice play skills with a peer.

Like any other goal, peer interaction should be taught in achievable steps. If turn-taking is a goal in your child's program, the therapist may teach this skill in a very discrete, structured manner. As your child gains skills and can demonstrate turn-taking with the therapist, the focus will shift from a more discrete teaching style to a more natural one, with siblings taking the role the therapist once played. The therapist will still be actively involved in the session by modeling behavior and prompting your child (or his sibling) when necessary.

It's important to recognize that the ABA therapist might have serious reservations about allowing a sibling to share the session. Sometimes, we can see that data can become skewed when influenced by a sibling. Having a sibling in the session also prevents the therapist from giving their full attention to your child with autism. Above all, the ABA therapist wants your child to accomplish as much as possible in the short period of time they have to teach them.

10. Can I videotape the session? Can I install a live feed?

It depends. Some agencies do not permit sessions to be videotaped or photographed under any circumstances, and others may be very open to the idea. If you would like a portion of the session to be videotaped, you may need to submit a written request to the agency, and the case supervisor may need to be present.

Sometimes, a supervisor may videotape your child to have a record of their progress, or to use to give feedback to the behavioral specialist. The case supervisor should notify you of their intention to occasionally videotape session.

11. I've noticed that my therapist takes
my child outside to play as part of the
session. Isn't this a waste of time?

One of the most difficult things for children with autism
are transitions between events. Abruptly ending a TV
show to eat dinner might lead to a major meltdown for
certain children. For this reason, the ABA therapist will
include a break or two during session. This allows your
child the opportunity to leave session and return. Some
children do this with no protests, or don't even want to
take a break. Other children think that session and the
demands of the session are over, and aren't pleased to
return. The transition back to session is an opportunity
for your child to experience transitions in a relatively
controlled environment, and to learn to self-soothe if they
are unhappy.

Your therapist may also be using playtime outside as
another environment to practice skills in. He or she might
be encouraging eye contact before throwing a ball, or
testing how well your child follows verbal directions. If
you are unsure of the purpose of the outside playtime, ask
your therapist. They will probably even give you some
great ideas to use on your own.

12. I noticed that my child's ABA
therapist spends 20 minutes or so
doing paperwork. Why is this?

All ABA therapists need to spend time before and after
session reviewing your child's progress, writing notes,
and taking care of other "housekeeping" paperwork
tasks. If you look through the binder, you will probably
see a sign-in sheet, behavior documentation pages, and

individual program progress and goals. All of these pages need to be completed carefully and accurately. When the behavior therapist is completing paperwork, they are also analyzing the data to determine if your child may move to the next level of the program. At the beginning of the session, they will also review the data to determine if your child mastered a program with another therapist. These frequent program reviews are very important. If your child's therapist doesn't notice that your child has mastered identifying the label "zebra," then they won't move the program on to the next step. The ABA therapist wants your child to move forward through their program as quickly as possible, so it's especially important for them to review and analyze the data frequently.

13. I noticed that my child's ABA session usually includes some time spent at the table. Can you tell me why they do so much work there?

Working at a small table accomplishes several purposes. There are several compliance and attention goals that your child may have included in their program, and the use of a table and chair provides an opportunity for the ABA therapist to include them. Your child may be working on:

- Compliance—coming and sitting at the table when asked, or returning to the table after a play break.

- Play Skills—choosing a toy to play with while on a break from working.

- Attending—focusing on a task and ignoring distractions.

- Behavior—leaving a non-preferred activity on the table (instead of sweeping it off onto the floor, for instance).

Additionally, teaching your child to sit at a table appropriately, attend to a teacher, and stay until excused will help prepare them for school. Finally, many new skills are introduced at the table and then generalized into the natural environment as your child progresses. As your child progresses in her ABA program, you may see less of a focus of learning at the table and more in the natural environment.

14. I keep offering my ABA therapist a meal, and they always refuse. Why are they so rude?

Any therapist who enters your home should be polite, friendly, and attentive to you and your child. They should behave in a professional, businesslike manner and will set and maintain appropriate boundaries. For most educators, this means limiting social interactions with clients. This maximizes instructional time and prevents the session from going off track. Aside from birthday cake, the ABA therapist probably won't share a meal with you (at least while they are actively involved in your child's case). In some cases, the ABA therapist may model eating for your child, especially if they have a very restricted diet or other eating behaviors.

15. I thought my child would really like this. Instead, he cries frequently during session. What's wrong?

ABA therapy programs always begin with a period of assessment and rapport building between the therapist and your child. For those first few days, the session is super fun! The ABA therapist wants your child to think of the therapist's presence in the home as a fun thing! But gradually, the therapist will place demands on your child. It's important for your child to learn to work through their displeasure and still be able to stay at the table, follow directions, and adapt to a learning environment. All these skills will come into play when your child enters the school system, and you'll be surprised at how so many of the tasks your child was doing begin to make sense. Give it time. The therapist knows that it's difficult to hear your child cry, and they can give you more information about what to expect during sessions, including ways to learn to ignore problem behavior and easy techniques to use that will help reinforce the skills they are learning in session.

16. My child cried a lot during his last session. It made me feel really stressed out! What should I do?

Remember, children participating in an in-home ABA therapy program may cry from time to time, and the ABA therapist is an expert in judging whether or not their crying is excessive or perhaps caused by something other than dislike of the demands of the session. If the ABA therapist is ignoring the crying and continuing to work, follow their lead. Don't interrupt the session and "rescue" your child. The worst thing you can do if your child is engaged in a serious tantrum is run into the room with a cookie. Sure, the crying will stop, as your child takes bites of the cookie and cuddles with you. But what you have really done is positively reinforce the crying: When your child cried, you introduced a reinforcer that increases the likelihood that that behavior will occur in a similar way in the future. Now, your child has learned that if he cries hard enough and long enough, a cookie will eventually be presented.

What you CAN do is be prepared for your child to cry. Be prepared for them to cry and for it to tear at your heartstrings. But there are simple things you can do that will help you get through it:

- read a book

- do a crossword puzzle

- do a chore like dishes, laundry, or tidying up the house

- research something on the computer

- prepare the next week's recipes.

Simply put, you should have five go-to activities that you can immediately turn to when your child is crying, and you know that you need to ignore that behavior. These activities can be used not just during session times. All children will cry with the hope that their tears will sway their parents. If you are prepared with an immediate way to distract yourself, those tantrums will become easier and easier to ignore.

CHAPTER 3

Outside of Sessions

Vignette: Marta and Sawyer

. . . .

Marta and eight-year-old Sawyer visit the park every
weekend. Although Sawyer is seven years old, he
is non-verbal and communicates primarily through
gestures. He also has a difficult time attending to tasks
and interacting with others. He has been practicing
these skills in his regular ABA sessions and Marta has
been trying to continue teaching these skills outside
of sessions.

When Marta and Sawyer arrive at the park, Marta
is pleased to see that the man with the ice cream
cart has already set up. She knows that he is patient
and kind, and has helped Sawyer before. Marta asks
Sawyer if he wants ice cream, and Sawyer nods. Marta
tucks a $5 bill into Sawyer's shorts and walks with
him to the ice cream man. Waiting in line is hard for

Sawyer. He wanders away several times and needs to be physically directed back. When it is Sawyer's turn at last, the ice cream vendor places two different cones on the top of the cooler and asks him, "What do you want today?" Sawyer takes out the $5 bill and gives it to the man. Marta gently takes it back, puts it into Sawyer's pocket, and says, "Sawyer, which one do you want?" Sawyer simply stands, looking down at the ice cream. Marta and the ice cream vendor make eye contact, and he hands both cones to Marta. Marta holds both cones out to Sawyer, asks again "What do you want?" and waits for Sawyer's response. Sawyer reaches toward the chocolate cone. Marta says, "Ooohhh, you want chocolate! Yum." She points to her pocket, and Sawyer takes his money out and pays the vendor. When the ice cream man looks around the park a few minutes later, he can see Sawyer and his mom sitting beneath a tree, where Sawyer is enjoying his cone in the shade.

Marta knows that with a little extra time and patience, Sawyer can interact with friends and make choices, just as a verbal child would do. She has practiced with Sawyer ways to help him make a selection, which gives him the opportunity to try things with as little assistance as possible. When he needs a little help, Marta knows exactly what to do, and does just what he needs, nothing more. This enables Sawyer to be as independent as possible and helps him develop even more independence skills.

1. What should I do outside of sessions?

This depends on the specific goals of your child's program. The team will tell you specifically what to do. If your child has a counting goal, you can practice that during playtime, by counting blocks, army men, or puzzle pieces. Is following directions one of your child's goals? If so, you can ask your child to retrieve something from the kitchen, put something away, or go to a specific area of the house. Children who are extremely sensitive to textures or smells may spend time outside of session playing with putty or touching wet sand. The possibilities are endless, and if you are unsure how to continue your child's learning outside of session, ask your therapist for specific ideas. Ideally, you will know at least one way to practice a skill that is DIFFERENT from how it is done during session, for each skill area.

2. My child really likes the toys the therapist uses. Should I go out and buy them?

A therapist's job is made much easier when he uses toys that are novel and grab the attention of the child they are working with. Even though building an eight-block tower isn't particularly fun for Bobby, it's much more enjoyable when he knows he will be able to play with a powerful reinforcer when he is done. If Bobby has access to every possible toy, none of them will be novel enough to motivate. For that reason, you should refrain from purchasing Bobby's favorite ABA toy.

However, there may be an occasion that the ABA therapist recommends that you buy a toy, with instructions to keep it novel. A great example of this is a super fun toy used only when Bobby is sitting quietly in the shopping cart at the grocery store.

3. Why should the toys be unavailable outside of session times?

Almost nothing is more discouraging than an ABA therapist coming to their regularly scheduled session, only to find that the bin has been opened, toys are scattered everywhere, and papers are ripped out of the binder. We want to keep your child motivated and excited by the prospect of having a session. When the therapist enters with their big bag of toys, or the bin is dragged out of the closet, we want your child to light up and get excited! Session will feel more like playtime to your child if they have no access to the toys during non-session times. There may also be times where the therapist will "retire" a toy for a week or two, in order to give your child a break from it, especially if it's becoming an obsession, OR if they simply want to recreate the novelty of the toy. Your child will be more successful if you follow your therapist's advice and keep those fun toys hidden away.

4. I'd like to buy my child some new toys, but he seems to be very distracted by flashing lights and noises. Should I go ahead and buy these types of toys?

Every child with autism is different, and they each have their own method and style of playing. Sometimes, certain toys may turn into obsessions, or simply be distracting. Toys with blinking lights and loud noises may have no impact whatsoever on certain children, and may lead others to play with them inappropriately, engaging in stereotypical behaviors (staring into the lights, for example). If you notice that your child is playing with any toy inappropriately (read: in a way that it was not intended), simply remove the toy and "retire" it for several days. Then, reintroduce the toy and watch for those stereotypical behaviors. You may need to teach your child the appropriate way to play with a toy. You can even "retire" the toy for weeks or months, and reintroduce it at another time. You will soon get a feel for what toys will work and what toys increase or contribute to stereotypic behaviors.

I have occasionally used my set of teeny-tiny screwdrivers to take apart toys that have one or two blinking components that distract students. Usually, you can find the wire that supplies power to the light, and either disconnect it or sever it entirely. If you sever it, it will NEVER WORK AGAIN! If you disconnect it, it may NEVER WORK AGAIN! Consider this your warning if you attempt any toy modifications.

5. What is "stimming"? How can I prevent it?

Some children with autism engage in self-stimulatory, stereotyped behaviors such as turning in circles, repetitively rolling cars back and forth, or hand flapping. The word "stimming" is a non-behavioral term that most ABA professionals try to avoid. They prefer to refer to those behaviors as "stereotyped" or "repetitive." Why? Well, it's just more professional and appropriate to use behavioral language to refer to behavioral issues.

One of the most frequently asked questions about self-stimulatory behaviors is how to identify them, and how to interrupt them. I always tell parents that even typical children engage in repetitive behaviors. Children with autism, however, might take these repetitive behaviors to another level. A toddler with autism might fill up a cup with blocks, dump it on the table, then refill the cup and do it all over again. If your child is engaged in meaningful play with a toy, and that play doesn't look to be repetitive, it's probably not. If you notice that your child is playing with toys not in the way they were intended, such as dropping a toy car onto the tile floor over and over, that is probably a stereotyped behavior that we don't want to encourage. You can interrupt a stereotyped behavior by showing your child the appropriate way to play with the toy (such as rolling that car along the floor), or you can block that behavior to prevent it. Moving from the tile kitchen to a carpeted bedroom might end the car-dropping behavior, because the noise of the car bouncing off the tile won't be present.

6. My therapist gave me their cell phone number, but instructed me to call the office first if I needed to cancel. Shouldn't I just call them directly?

ABA agencies vary in how much access they give parents to the therapist's contact information. Some agencies never provide any therapist contact information to parents, asking instead that they contact the agency scheduler or program supervisor with any changes. However, many independent contractors make their own schedules and will gladly provide their cell phone numbers. If you have your ABA therapist's contact information, treat it as you would any business professional. Call them only during business hours and be mindful that they may not be able to return your call until the following business day. If you have an emergency, please call the ABA agency office directly.

7. Can I just text my child's ABA therapist, or email them?

Probably. Some ABA therapists might actually prefer text messages. Email is also a great way to get information to your ABA therapist or to the program supervisor, but remember, never consider information you send via email to be secure and private. You may want to consider using your child's initials instead of their full name.

8. My husband and I are having problems. Should I talk to my ABA therapist about it?

Nope. They aren't that kind of therapist. In fact, unless personal information is relevant to your child's case, we really don't want to know. By all means, inform the case supervisor and the team if major changes are happening in the home, such as the entrance or exit of a family member, loss of a pet, separation or divorce, or things of that nature. These more serious events can definitely affect your child's behavior, and it's nice to let the team know that these things are happening. However, nobody on the ABA team, including the case supervisor, is qualified or ethically allowed to counsel your family on non-case-related issues.

9. Can my ABA therapist and I be friends?

Being an ABA therapist is a unique job. An ABA therapist spends the majority of their day working with children, sometimes with little parent interaction, and because of the independent nature of ABA therapy, sometimes the only other adults an ABA therapist sees are parents. Professionals in every regard, an ABA therapist is responsible for maintaining confidentiality and a professional relationship with every family they work with. It can be difficult to maintain a professional relationship with families. Parent interaction is vital to the success of the program, and it is important that the therapist maintain a professional relationship with the family. Simply said, it will be easier for the therapist to make decisions that impact the future of your child if they are NOT in your circle of friends. That being said, it's entirely appropriate (and polite) to ask your ABA therapist how their weekend was, wish them happy holidays, or ask if they would like a drink or if they would like to use your bathroom.

When it is time for your child to leave the ABA program, you may certainly express your desire to stay in contact with the therapist. They will let you know if they are interested in remaining in contact. Remember, though, that an amazing therapist can be hard to come by, and if there is a chance you may want to use the services of the therapist later, you might want to seriously consider keeping the relationship strictly professional.

10. I found my ABA therapist on Facebook! Should I add him to my friend list?

Although social networks give tempting access to business professionals such as your ABA team, refrain from "friending" them. You would probably be putting them in an uncomfortable situation. Keep the relationship professional, just as you would that of a doctor or dentist. Instead, ask if their agency has a social networking page, and join that group instead. If they don't have one, ask if they can create one. You surely won't be the only parent who wants to have online social networking contact with their ABA team.

11. Can I ask my ABA therapist to babysit for me or do therapy "under the table"?

Nope. Sorry, but there are several reasons for this. First of all, many ABA agencies have strict no-competition clauses in their contracts with employees. This means that the employee is prohibited from working for another agency, school, or family where they will be providing ABA therapy not through their agency. By asking your ABA therapist to babysit or provide respite, you may be unwittingly asking them to violate their contract with their employer.

12. Why does my child seem to attend to lessons so well, but doesn't listen to me? What can I do to get my child to behave?

Sessions with your child's ABA provider are highly structured, and designed to have a minimum of distraction and interruption. The ABA therapist is also an expert in ignoring bad behavior, and they usually have years of experience in dealing with all types of problem behavior. I always say that I can be "immune" to certain behaviors, because as an ABA therapist, I can leave after two hours and those behaviors no longer affect me. When the ABA therapist is a bit detached from the child and their behaviors, it is easier to stick to the behavior program and change problem behaviors.

This doesn't mean that your child will attend to sessions, have great behavior, and it all flies out the front door when the therapist leaves. While the ABA therapist wants to see your child gain skills and develop more adaptive behaviors, their number one priority is teaching you, the parent, how to maintain these new skills in the absence of a therapy session. This is just one of the many reasons that the therapist will require that you be actively involved in sessions, and if you feel that you aren't learning enough skills, or you have questions in regards with how to handle specific behavior, tell your therapist. There are many behaviors that aren't specifically dealt with in session, such as feeding or sleeping, that the ABA agency can help you with! Just let them know what you need and they can design a behavioral intervention to address these problem behaviors.

PART 2

Programming, Lingo, and Data Collection

CHAPTER 4

Tailoring the ABA Program

Vignette: Saul Lee

Saul Lee is a six-year-old Chinese boy with autism. His family is living in Los Angeles for an extended period of time, while his father works at a software development company. A Chinese family with deep traditional roots, the Lee family always removes their shoes when entering the home. Saul enters the house, runs upstairs, and ignores repeated shouted requests from his parents to come back downstairs and take off his shoes.

During his monthly in-home clinic meeting, Saul's parents told the team about their difficulties in teaching Saul to remove his shoes while at home. The program supervisor then developed a program that taught Saul the steps he needed to take when he returned home from an outing. He learned to sit down on a mat on the floor, remove his shoes and where to place them on a nearby shelf. His parents learned how to properly request that Saul remove his shoes, how to assist him if necessary, and better ways to communicate with Saul. When the family returned home to China, Saul was able to maintain his new skill.

. . . .

1. How does the team decide what goals are appropriate for my child?

Before the ABA program begins, the program supervisor will meet with you as part of the assessment process. They will ask detailed questions on every aspect of your child's life, gaining information regarding feeding, eye contact, play and social skills, toileting, compliance, and much more. The program supervisor will also observe your child, and may accompany you on an outing. From these observations and interviews, they will develop a preliminary plan for programming. As your child becomes more accustomed to the ABA team, the programming goals will be frequently evaluated and changed if necessary.

I recently developed a goal for a student, who, although verbal, did not respond audibly when called by his mother. He had become lost in a department store, and did not respond to his mother's calls. She related this story to me, and we immediately decided to add a goal that would work to increase the volume and amount of her son's verbal responses to his mother's calls. Now, when someone calls, "Brandon", he will attempt to respond with "What?", or

"Here I am!" This is just one example of ways to tailor an ABA program for a child's individual needs.

2. How can such simple play activities help my child learn and achieve his educational and behavioral goals?

At first glance, it might seem that blowing bubbles and rolling a ball back to the therapist are strictly play skills. However, look closer.

Vignette: John and Annie

John, an ABA therapist from Chicago, is working with Annie, a non-verbal two year old. John sits in front of Annie, dips a wand into bubble solution, and, while making eye contact with Annie, says "One, two, …" When Annie makes eye contact, John says "Three!" and blows the bubbles. Annie loves this game and soon learns that after John says "One, two", she will need to make eye contact to make John say "Three!" and blow the bubbles. Notice that the therapist holds off on blowing the bubble wand until Annie has made eye contact. In time, John will require more and more of Annie before blowing those bubbles. Soon, John will encourage Annie to make any kind of vocalization before he will blow the bubbles. As Annie gains these skills in vocalizing, John will shape her vocalizations into the word "Three", by reinforcing her closer and closer attempts at the word.

Each task that the therapist does with your child is related to a specific goal. It probably looks like they are just playing, however, they are working hard on various educational, social, and play skills. There are many different goal areas for ABA programming. Some are listed in Table 4.1, along with the types of activities that the therapist may use to practice them.

Table 4.1 ABA goals and related activities

Goal Area	Activity
Problem solving	Puzzles, nesting cups, ring stacker on graduated cone
Compliance	Come sit down, go play, give to me
Task completion skills	Puzzles, string beads, placing pegs into holes
Sensory-based activities	Touching, squeezing, or poking putty, reaching into a bin filled with rice or beans to retrieve a toy
Play skills	Sharing, taking turns, eye contact, learning simple games
Imitation	Knock table, cover eyes, clap, tap thighs, tap table, stomp feet, arms up, turn around, nod head, shake head, jump, stand up, wave, high-five, blow kiss
Cognitive tasks	Matching colors, shapes, objects, or categories, expressively or receptively labeling vehicles, toys, food, clothing, etc.

3. I have seen other children using a photo communication system. Does this really work? Can it help my child?

Photo communication systems are another technique found in the ABA "toolbox." They use photo cards or icons to help non-verbal people communicate. The photo cards or icons are usually placed on the cover of a three-ring binder, with additional photos and icons inside. As your child progresses through the various levels of the photo communication system, they will become more able to communicate their wants and needs independently. If you are implementing this type of communication system at home, be sure that it is in place in every environment your child is in, including school and daycare. Also, make sure that everyone your child is involved with is implementing the system in exactly the same manner! If you and the school are using the system in the same way, but the daycare provider puts the book away as soon as your son arrives, it's not going to work as well as it should.

4. What if I have ideas for the program?

Parents and caregivers are the number one source of information about both the abilities and challenges faced by their child. ABA programs may include academic, self-help, and social skills goals. If you have an idea for a specific skill you would like your child to work on, or if you aren't sure why the program includes a certain task, share that with the ABA team. Your input is extremely important in determining programming goals.

5. How can ABA be used to help with challenging behavior?

ABA uses the principles of reinforcement to change behavior. That is, by reinforcing a behavior we want, we are increasing the likelihood that that behavior will happen more in the future. By failing to reinforce a behavior that we previously DID reinforce, we are decreasing the likelihood that that behavior will occur more in the future. Let's look at an example:

Vignette: Heather and Jayden

. . . .

Heather has a six-year-old son, Jayden. Jayden frequently interrupts Heather when she is on the phone. On Monday, the phone rang, and Heather answered. Almost immediately, Jayden put down his book and ran over to Heather, asking loudly for a cookie. Heather turns her back and tries to continue her conversation. Jayden, not to be deterred, takes off his shoe and throws it at the kitchen cabinet. Then he falls to the floor, kicking and screaming. Heather, needing to complete this important work phone call, relents and gives Jayden half of a cookie. He immediately quiets down and returns to his book.

The next day, Heather discusses Jayden's behavior with his ABA therapist. The therapist recommends "extinction," a program where all aspects of an undesirable behavior are ignored, and other behaviors that are substitutes for the undesirable behavior are rewarded. The therapist schedules a call with Heather for 4:30 that evening, just before Heather and Jayden usually eat dinner. Again, Heather answers the phone and turns her back to Jayden when he runs over, asking for a pudding cup. This time, the therapist talks Heather through fully ignoring Jayden's demands. Heather makes no eye contact with Jayden and does not respond when he removes his shirt and throws it at her. In fact, Heather walks away from Jayden every time he approaches her. Eventually, Jayden gives up and returns to his bedroom. Jayden and Heather eat dinner on schedule, and Heather praises Jayden for his good behavior at the table. They share a pudding cup for dessert.

• •

You can see how Jayden used his behavior to influence the behavior of his mother. The phone ringing and Heather answering set the stage for Jayden's behavior of asking for a cookie, crying, and tantruming. When he asked for the cookie, and Heather said, "No," Jayden "upped the ante" by increasing his volume and intensity of his behavior. When Heather gave in to him and handed him a cookie, she inadvertently reinforced the very behavior she was trying to stop. Scheduling a time for the therapist to call Heather provided an ideal time to practice the skills needed for Heather to implement the extinction procedure on her own. By sticking with it, Heather will be able to teach Jayden to approach her during phone calls appropriately (such as a light tap to her shoulder), and to wait until she is done for less important needs.

6. How can ABA be used to help with play skills?
Sounds funny, right? All kids know how to play, don't they? The answer, at least for some children with autism,

is a clear "No." Children learn a lot about play and how to interact by observing and imitating other children, and children with autism may have deficits in imitation skills. When presented with a doll and a toy bottle, a child with autism may not know what to do, even if they have seen another child or adult "feed" the baby before.

How does ABA address these play skill deficits? Play skills are easy to add to a program, teach, and maintain. An in-home ABA program can teach play skills that can be done alone (such as completing a puzzle or putting balls through a ball drop toy) and pretend play skills, as well as a range of other play-related skills like turn-taking, emotions, and following directions. In the case of a child who does not know how to play appropriately with a baby doll, the therapist may start with a specific instruction, such as "Do this," and then model feeding the baby. Children with more advanced play skills may be given a more general instruction. During a break from work, the therapist may give the instruction, "Go play," and will observe and take data on your child's success in following this instruction. If your child simply goes and sits next to a toy and doesn't actively engage with it, the therapist will prompt your child to use the toy (or to use the toy appropriately, if necessary).

7. How can ABA be used to help with communication skills?

Imagine if you could not communicate your wants and needs to people. How would you signal that you are hungry? How would you indicate that you are tired of playing a game? From basic needs such as food, drink, and warmth, to more advanced conversational skills, ABA can help teach your child to become a more independent communicator. Specific programs may be developed to teach a child to request a desired object or activity, to cease an activity, or to comment on objects or topics. This may be done with the collaboration of a speech professional, such as a Speech Language Pathologist (SLP), for instance.

8. How can ABA be used to help with motor skills?

Fine and gross motor skills can also be included in an in-home ABA program. Sometimes, an occupational therapist or physical therapist is part of the team and develops goals designed to target specific motor deficits.

Fine motor skills are those that involve the small muscles of the body. In addition to the goals developed by these specialized professionals, the therapist and supervisor may work on fine motor skills as well. For example, tasks that fit under the category of "task completion," such as completing a puzzle, stringing wooden beads on a stick or string, and placing a peg in a hole are all examples of tasks that assist in the development of fine motor skills AND task completion skills. You may also see fine motor skills developed in programs that require your child to draw, color, cut, or lace.

Gross motor skills are those that involve the large muscles of the body. You see gross motor skills when you observe a child running, jumping, bending over, pumping his legs on the swing, etc. Children who have deficits in gross motor skills might have tasks built into their in-home program that target these needed skills. A child may take a break to jump on a trampoline, practice kicking a ball, or hop on one foot.

9. My child has sensory processing issues. How will the therapist take this into consideration?

Many parents of children with autism report that they show a dislike for certain smells, tastes, or textures. In fact, numerous ABA agencies introduce programs to almost all their clients that help them assess these sensory needs. Sometimes, the therapist may offer the child a bit of lotion and demonstrate how to rub it into the hands. You may see times where the therapist brings shaving cream or pudding to session, with the intent of having your child "paint" with it. Or, you may see that your child has a task that involves clay or dough. In the beginning of therapy, the therapist will ask your child to simply touch the clay or dough. Later tasks will involve poking, patting, or squeezing it. You may be surprised…many children who showed a real aversion to such textures go on to play effortlessly with it, and even graduate to touching slime!

Of course, if your child is extremely distressed by touching or poking dough, shaving cream, or pudding, the therapist will not force him to interact with these items. I have known several children who became distressed when clay or dough was even present in the room, and became even more upset when the lid was taken off the container. Children with this level of sensitivity to dough will first learn to accept the dough being in the room, then on the table (in the container), and finally, may even be willing to interact with it. That first interaction may be with the dough being inside a plastic bag, but it still is a first step. If your child has specific sensory sensitivities, let your therapist know. They can program into your child's schedule activities that will get them used to various textures, at the same time teaching your child valuable play and academic skills.

10. My ABA therapist wants to use "video modeling" with my child. What is this?

Video modeling is a method of teaching that uses observation of video-recorded behaviors that are then imitated by the student. The target behavior is first learned, then memorized, imitated, and finally, generalized to new settings. Video modeling enables students to watch a precise behavior as many times as necessary. Skills recorded during video modeling can be broken down into the most basic steps, giving the student the chance to see exactly how the behavior is done.

How might video modeling be used within an ABA session? Imagine that your child has a tooth-brushing task. He puts a tiny bit of toothpaste on his brush, licks it off, and drinks his cup of water. His ABA therapist may video record himself, your child, or a sibling doing the specific steps correctly, in the correct order. Then, the video is shown to your child. It will show video examples of the following steps:

1. Take toothbrush from cup.

2. Pick up toothpaste.

3. Remove cap of toothpaste.

4. Squeeze pea-sized amount onto head of toothbrush.

5. Place cap back on toothpaste.

6. Wet brush under water.

7. Turn water off.

8. Brush front teeth.

9. Brush left side upper.

10. Brush left side lower.

11. Brush right side upper.

12. Brush right side lower.

13. Brush tongue.

14. Spit toothpaste into sink.

15. Turn water back on.

16. Fill cup with water.

17. Turn off water.

18. Fill mouth with water.

19. Swish water in mouth.

20. Spit water into sink.

21. Turn water on.

22. Rinse brush under water.

23. Turn water off.

24. Replace brush into cup.

25. Dry hands.

You can see how many steps there are to tooth brushing, and how important it is to do them in the correct order. Video modeling is useful for teaching many tasks in your child's ABA program.

CHAPTER 5

Learning the Lingo

Vignette: Patrick and Dawn

Patrick and his two-year-old daughter have been working with an in-home ABA agency for three weeks. One weekend, Patrick opens up the bin of toys, takes out the program binder, and begins to read through the notes. Whew! He is completely confused by strings of information such as "C, I, PP, C, C, NR, HOH, PP, GP, C = 40 percent." He finds pages in the binder titled "A-B-C Data," "Bx Frequency Count," and "Goals on Maintenance." Patrick wonders what all the letters and words mean and searches through the binder for a legend. Finding nothing, he puts the bin away and makes a mental note to ask the therapist just what all that nonsense is.

1. I hear a lot about the A-B-Cs in ABA. What is this?

A-B-C stands for Antecedent, Behavior, and Consequence.

To better understand this, it's helpful to learn that all behavior follows the same path: Antecedent, behavior, and consequence. Let's look at an example:

Sue is a three-year-old girl with autism who has just begun an ABA program. When Sue's mother gives her an eight-piece wooden knob puzzle to complete, Sue typically throws the pieces, chews on them, or bangs them on the table. During her session, Sue's mom watches as Freddy, her therapist, lays a wooden knob puzzle down on the table with only one piece missing. Sue ignores the puzzle until Freddy says, "Finish the puzzle." Sue picks up the missing piece and tries to fit it in the correct place. Freddy guides her hand gently until the puzzle piece falls into place, then immediately bursts into a wide grin, high-fives Sue, and gives her a small piece of potato chip from a nearby bag. Sue grins and claps. What just happened? Let's look at it in a simpler form:

Antecedent	Behavior	Consequence
Freddy says, "Finish the puzzle."	Sue picks up the puzzle piece and, with help, fits it into the correct space.	Freddy's big smile, his high-five, and a piece of potato chip.

Sue's behavior has just been changed by the consequence that happened: When she completed the puzzle, Freddy smiled, gave her a high-five, and she got to eat a piece of her favorite food. Over time, as Sue is repeatedly rewarded for completing the puzzle, we will see her behavior of placing the puzzle piece in the correct place increase, even without the potato chips being present.

How this all relates to your child and ABA is simple: By tracking ABC data, you can gain a better understanding of things that happen before a behavior, and after. Analyzing this data helps you see trends in behavior that you can manipulate to change a behavior. This first example showed how we can use the principles of reinforcement to increase a behavior.

Now, let's look at another example.

Brandi has been Sarah's ABA therapist for over a year. One day, Sarah's mom mentions that Sarah has a new behavior, one of removing food from the kitchen trashcan and eating it. Sarah's mom has been reprimanding Sarah for attempting to eat the trash, and has resorted to placing the trashcan on the top of the refrigerator in order to prevent Sarah from reaching it. Despite her mom's efforts, Sarah seems increasingly interested in the contents of the trashcan, and has begun to remove non-edible items as well, and has attempted to climb to the top of the refrigerator to access it.

Brandi leaves a A-B-C chart with Sarah's mom, with instructions to complete it as Sarah exhibits the behaviors of eating food from the trash can or climbing to reach it. At Brandi's next weekly session, she reviews the A-B-C chart, which has been carefully filled in by Sarah's mom:

Antecedant	Behavior	Consequence
Food placed in the trash can after dinner.	Sarah goes to the trash can 20 minutes after she has been excused from the table, and tries to eat the food.	I asked Sarah if she was still hungry, and when she nodded, I gave her a small snack.

Brandi immediately sees that, while well-meaning, Sarah's mother may be maintaining Sarah's behavior by giving her a treat after dinner. Although further data needs to be gathered, Brandi begins thinking about ways that Sarah could appropriately ask for more food, gain attention from her mother, and increase her consumption of food at dinner.

2. What is positive reinforcement?

Positive reinforcement is anything that follows a behavior that increases the likelihood that that behavior will occur again, in the same way, in the future. Think of the "positive" part of positive reinforcement literally, as a +, meaning that you are ADDING something to the behavioral equation. If you present a child with three blocks, give the instruction, "Build a tower", and then immediately reinforce the child with a piece of candy (there is the +), AND that reinforcement makes the behavior more likely to occur in the future, you have just used positive reinforcement. Another example may hit a bit closer to home: You go to work early and stay later all month, which increases your sales numbers. At the end of the month, you have earned a $500 bonus (again, there is the +) from your employer! Are you more likely to go in to work early and stay late in the future? If so, that $500 acts as a positive reinforcer.

Positive reinforcement, however, doesn't always mean that the behavior it reinforces is one that is desired. If, for example, your child tantrums in the grocery store, begging for a toy, and you give in and purchase that toy (the +), you are positively reinforcing that behavior! As you can see, the term "positive reinforcement" has more to do with the likelihood of the behavior occurring again in the future, not necessarily our desire to see that behavior again.

3. How does the ABA therapist determine what to use as a reinforcer?

Every child has different preferences, and even children who absolutely love trains, for instance, will probably lose interest in that and move on to something else. For this reason, the ABA therapist will frequently assess what most motivates your child. This usually takes place at the beginning of session, and may be as simple as the therapist placing three toys in front of your child, and tracking which toy they choose first, then second, and then third. The therapist will then use those toys as reinforcers for the session. If your child is working on a particularly difficult or new task, and does very well, the therapist will reward your child with the most preferred reinforcer. If they perform so-so, then the therapist will probably offer them the second preferred reinforcer. If they have a tough time with the task, they will probably be offered their least preferred reinforcer.

4. My child LOVES candy. Can't we use that as a reinforcer?

Edible reinforcers, such as candy, chips, or sips of a preferred drink are considered *primary reinforcers*. These reinforcers are best described as something that a person cannot live without. Examples of primary reinforcers are food, water, and warmth. If your child loves candy, and it is more reinforcing than any other item such as a toy, the therapist may choose to use candy as a reinforcer, with the aim of replacing it with a more appropriate reinforcer, such as a toy. If your ABA therapist is using candy as a reinforcer, they will always pair it with verbal praise, so that eventually your child will be as reinforced by verbal praise as they are by candy. For edible reinforcers to be most effective, your child should have limited access to their preferred edible reinforcer. This might mean only using their preferred edible reinforcer during session times, and ensuring that they are not full from a recent meal. In order to keep the reinforcer motivating, the therapist will provide limited access to it (i.e. allowing a pea-sized piece of chip or cookie for each reward). The ABA team should always discuss their desire to use food reinforcers with you before beginning this as a technique. Over the long term, the use of edible reinforcers is best faded, as some schools have restrictions on the type and usage of food in a classroom.

5. What is "extinction"?

Extinction is a procedure where reinforcement for a previously reinforced behavior is withheld and the frequency of the behavior decreases. For example, consider a child who frequently climbs the shelves in the pantry to get a cookie from the top shelf, where mom has "hidden" them. The climbing behavior is reinforced with cookies. If mom stops buying cookies all together, when the child climbs the shelves, he will not be reinforced because no cookies (or other treats) are there. Eventually he will decrease or even stop climbing the shelves due to lack of reinforcement.

This is extinction.

One side effect is what is known as an "extinction burst" where a behavior may temporarily become worse before it gets better. Consider a child who throws tantrums until his mom finally consoles him and gives him some ice cream to make him feel better. When the practitioner recommends that mom stops consoling him and offering him ice cream (extinction), he begins tantruming even harder, longer, and louder than ever before. Think about it; He has always gotten hugs from mom and ice cream when he tantrumed in the past, so when those things are withheld, he is going to try even harder to get them. This is called an extinction burst. If reinforcement continues to be withheld, not only will the extinction burst end, but also the behavior will continue to reduce.

Extinction can become tricky when other factors may inadvertently reinforce behavior. This is often the case when practitioners attempt to use extinction for behaviors that are reinforced by attention, or rather, by the reaction of others. For example, consider a child who throws things in the home in an effort to get his mother's attention. Prior to the intervention, every time he threw something, she would scold him and have him pick it up. Then, the practitioner recommends "putting the child on extinction" and recommends that the mother simply ignore the throwing behavior as if it didn't occur. This is a flawed attempt at extinction because when Aunt Edie comes over and little Jimmy throws his sippy cup at her, will she know she is supposed to ignore it? Probably not. When you and little Jimmy are at the grocery store and he throws something off the shelf, are the other shoppers and employees going to ignore the throwing? Probably not. These occurrences of attention for throwing by Aunt

Edie and the folks in the grocery store are reinforcing Jimmy's throwing behavior so extinction is not the most appropriate procedure to use in this circumstance.

Read the following vignette. Can you identify the where extinction is used?

Vignette: Anderson

Anderson, a two-year-old boy with autism, usually does session in the front living room at his house. He seems to like running from the front room to the kitchen, located at the rear of the house. His therapist notices that he runs very closely to the wall, tilting his head to one side, and seems to look at one specific spot on the wall. Anderson sprints by the wall at every opportunity, and can get to within a quarter inch of his nose scraping the wall. After several weeks of decreasing his distance to the wall, Anderson crashes into the wall with his face and cries. He also seems to be even more interested in running by the wall! His ABA therapist suggests that the family block his access to the wall by placing a stack of large sofa cushions in front of it. The cushions force Anderson to slow down and quickly extinguish this behavior.

Within a day or so, Anderson finds a new spot on another wall and charges by that wall too. The family moves the cushions to block his access to it, and again the behavior ends. After several cushion rearrangements, Anderson stops running by walls and turns his attention to other things.

6. What is "chaining"? What is a "task analysis"?

Chaining and task analysis go hand in hand. Let's first talk about task analysis. Task analysis is when a more complex skill is broken down into simpler steps. Consider brushing teeth, or making a peanut butter and jelly sandwich. While these may seem like rather simple tasks, there are actually many steps to each: getting the toothpaste, getting the toothbrush, opening the toothpaste, applying toothpaste to the toothbrush, and so on. Once the skill is broken down into simpler steps, chaining is used to teach each step individually and to link those steps together to ultimately teach the larger skill.

You may hear of "forward chaining" or "backward chaining." These terms simply refer to the direction in which the larger skill is taught. Forward chaining begins with teaching the first step and assisting the child with the remaining steps. Once the child masters the first step, the teaching will focus on the second step, and so on until the entire skill is mastered. Backward chaining is similar except the child is assisted through all steps, with the last step being the focus of the teaching. "Total task chaining" may also be used where teaching occurs during each step.

7. What is "prompting"?

Prompting refers to the level of assistance needed by your child to complete a task. For example, if you ask your child to put his or her plate in the sink, a prompt could take several forms. Your child could independently stand up, walk to the sink, and place the plate in the sink. You may have to point to the sink (gestural prompt), touch your child's arm or shoulder to turn him toward the sink (physical prompt), stand up and put your own plate away (model prompt), or physically assist your child in every step of the instruction: Standing up, picking up the plate, walking to the sink, and placing the plate in the sink (hand-over-hand prompt, or HOH prompt). Carefully used prompts help children learn new skills with a minimum of assistance. Prompts are faded as your child progresses, so that eventually, your child is completing tasks and following directions as independently as possible.

8. What is a "prompt dependency"?

Sometimes, children with autism or other behavioral disorders develop what is called prompt dependency. Children who are prompt dependent may know how to do a task, but will not begin to complete the task until they have been prompted. Because children with autism can become reliant on prompts, it is especially important to use prompts carefully, and always with the intention of fading them away. An ABA program that has been carefully designed and implemented will prevent or eliminate prompt dependency and can work to extinguish prompts that have already become part of your child's repertoire. Therapists who notice that a child who is reliant on prompts (during either session or non-session times) will make the appropriate changes that will decrease your child's need to rely on prompts, thus increasing their independence.

9. What is "fading"?

Fading has to do with prompting. Let's say that Joanie is learning to draw with a crayon. In the beginning, Joanie was not even the slightest bit interested in drawing with a crayon. Mark, her ABA therapist, had to physically motor Joanie's hand through the entire task of scribbling on paper. As mentioned above, this type of prompting is known as hand-over-hand prompting (or HOH). One day, Mark sees that Joanie made a move to pick up the crayon by herself. He took Joanie's hand, which had returned to her lap, and placed it over the crayon. Joanie picked it up and scribbled. Mark had automatically made the switch from HOH prompting to physical prompting. Mark will fade his physical prompts even more, from actually fully touching Joanie's hand to tapping it, to tapping her wrist, to tapping her elbow, to tapping her shoulder. Then, he may move to gestural prompts, simply pointing at the crayon or Joanie's hand.

ABA therapists are very, very aware of their prompts. The less intrusive the prompt, the better! We certainly don't want to HOH prompt a child if a gesture prompt will work. In addition, once we see that a child has the ability to complete a task at a less intrusive prompt level, we are hesitant to return to the more intrusive level. We are always aware of the prompt level we are working at and interested in how we can most quickly fade that prompt.

10. What is a "visual schedule"? How am I supposed to do this at home?

A visual schedule uses photos or icons to indicate a series of tasks or activities that are to be completed. You can also use a visual schedule to give information about a child's day, such as breakfast, bus, school, bus, and dentist appointment. It is usually designed in a vertical or horizontal format. Many visual schedules are designed to be used with a transition card that is given to the child and indicates the need to check their schedule. How does a transition card work? It's easy. A transition card can be a strip of paper, or even an object. When it is time for your child to move to the next step in their visual schedule, you simply hand them the transition card and help them find their schedule. Your child will take their transition card to the schedule, place it in a nearby envelope, and take the icon at the top of the schedule. That icon will travel with them to that activity. When it's time to move on to the next task, you simply repeat the process.

Transition cards and visual schedules work well at home and at school, and you can even make a portable one that you can take with you when you are out. They are a great visual tool!

Here's an example of how a visual schedule is being used for Andie, a fifth-grade girl.

11. What is an "open-ended task"?

An open-ended task is one that does not have a clear beginning or end. For example, placing a ring on a ring stacker has a clear beginning and end: The child picks up the ring and places it on the stick. Conversely, shaking a maraca or ringing a bell are tasks that are open-ended. A child can pick up a maraca and shake it indefinitely. There is no clear ending to the task. When used in an imitation program, closed-ended tasks are usually introduced first. Open-ended tasks are considered more difficult because the child has to make the decision to *stop* shaking the maraca or ringing the bell. Some children with autism have difficulty ending a task unless they are given a prompt. For this reason, the therapist will first teach closed-ended tasks first. When the child shows mastery of tasks such as stacking one block on top of another, putting a block in a bucket, or nesting two cups, the ABA therapist can move on to the more difficult open-ended skills.

Examples of open-ended tasks include:

- shake maraca
- ring bell
- pat, poke, or squeeze dough or putty
- clap hands
- knock on table
- turn around
- tap blocks or puzzle pieces together.

Examples of closed-ended tasks include:

- place a block in a bowl

- stack two blocks

- put ring on ring stacker

- put peg in pegboard

- nesting cups

- string beads.

12. What is "maintenance"?

When your child has mastered a particular skill, such as expressively identifying photos of farm animals, the therapist will maintain that task, that is, they will include those new skills in the ABA program and will periodically take data on them. It's important to maintain skills by periodically revisiting them and assessing your child's level of generalization. If the therapist notices that your child seems to have forgotten a skill that they had previously mastered, it will be reintroduced into your child's program.

13. What is a "probe" or "pre-test"?

A probe (or pre-test) is a way of testing a child to see what skills they have, what skills are emerging, and what skills need to be worked on. A probe can be used to check for maintenance of previously introduced skills, to see if students have generalized skills, or to test for knowledge of yet-to-be-introduced skills.

Table 5.1 gives examples of the probe technique used with Andie, a fifth-grade student, all taken during the same session.

Table 5.1 Examples of the probe techniques as used with Andie

Check for maintenance of previously introduced skills.	Time (digital) o'clock.	Upon probe, shows mastery of all previously mastered o'clock times.
Check for generalization.	Time (analog) o'clock.	Previously showed mastery of 12:00, 2:00, and 4:00. Upon teacher probe, Andie has clearly generalized her learning and has mastered all analog o'clock times.
Test for knowledge of yet-to-be-introduced skills.	Follow two-item picture clock schedule.	Upon probe, could not follow schedule.

14. What is an "expressive task"?

A task that requires the student to say or write something is considered an expressive task. When you hold up a picture of a monkey, and ask, "What is this?" you are targeting an expressive response.

15. What is a "receptive task"?

A task that asks a student to choose or otherwise indicate an answer is considered a receptive task. If you lay out three cards, and say, "Touch the clown," you are targeting a receptive response.

16. What is "sabotage"? Isn't this mean?

Sometimes, the ABA therapist may purposefully "sabotage" your child's success at a particular task. For example, when your child asks for a puzzle, the therapist may indeed give them a puzzle, but with the wrong pieces. The ABA therapist is trying to teach your child to identify what is wrong, look for the pieces, or ask for help if necessary. By pretending not to notice what is wrong, the therapist is creating a situation where your child needs to explain the situation or ask for help.

Another example of purposeful sabotage is trapping a desired item in an impossible-to-open container, asking groups of students to complete an art project with only one set of scissors, or hiding one shoe. These situations, set up in advance, work on problem solving and communication goals.

17. What is a "token economy"?

A token economy is a behavior technique that utilizes positive reinforcement. Students work for "tokens," such as stars, stickers, or plastic chips, which can later be exchanged for the reinforcer. The idea is that the student will earn a predetermined number of tokens before the reinforcer is offered. For every five tokens earned, for instance, the student will be given one piece of candy. For every 15 tokens earned, for example, the student earns 15 minutes of computer time. A token economy is an effective way to motivate students to learn new skills, encourage completion of tasks, and maintain skills already learned.

CHAPTER 6

It's All About the Data

Vignette: Annie and John

Annie is a behavioral therapist who has been working with three-year-old John for six months. The following describes their interaction during a work task:

John is sitting opposite Annie at a child-sized wooden table. Annie has a data sheet ready on a clipboard next to her, and a task prepared to present to John. Since John has only been working on this task for one week, Annie expects that she will probably need to prompt John to complete the task. For this task completion skill, John will be asked to string a bead. She waits until John makes eye contact with her, is sitting quietly, and appears ready to work. She then places a large wooden bead and a thick string onto the table, and says, "String the bead." John picks the bead up and places it on the string. Annie praises him and jots down a + in the right place on John's data sheet.

Annie puts another wooden bead on the table, and repeats her instruction, "String the bead." This time, John picks the bead up and drops it off the table. Annie records this as a - on John's data sheet, and immediately re-presents the bead to John. She says "String the bead," and this time assists John in guiding the large bead onto the string. After the bead is placed on the string, Annie says "Good job! Let's see if you can do one by yourself." She then gives John another bead, which he independently places on the string. Annie praises John, gives him a high-five, and hands him his favorite toy. Then, Annie writes a PP (see Table 6.1 on p.96) and a + on John's data sheet. John's data sheet now looks like this:

PROGRAM: STRING BEADS, ONE AT A TIME

1	2	3	4	5	6	7	8	9	10	%
+	-	PP	+							

After John plays with his toy for two minutes, Annie removes it and re-presents the task. She continues in this manner until she has completed ten trials. When Annie is finished, she counts up the number of correct responses and puts the data into percentage form. Now, John's data sheet looks like this:

PROGRAM: STRING BEADS, ONE AT A TIME

I	2	3	4	5	6	7	8	9	10	%
+	-	PP	+	-	PP	+	+	+	+	60%

· ·

Ugh. Data. That's probably what you think, right? Well, in the world of ABA, data is our best friend and behavior therapists take data on almost every aspect of an ABA session. Annie can easily evaluate John's progress on his task by a quick glance at his behavior. As your child progresses in their program and enters preschool and then kindergarten, you will see how data is invaluable to track your child's progress towards academic and behavior goals and evaluate behavioral interventions.

I. Why is data collection so important in ABA?

Applied behavior analysis is a scientific discipline that requires clear evidence of progress on goals in order to introduce new skills or make changes to existing programs. Although many in-home programs share similar characteristics, each in-home therapy program is specifically designed to help the child learn specific skills. Those skills are tracked and progress is measured through the data taken in session. In fact, you may see the therapist and the supervisor occasionally taking data on the same task. The data is calculated as a percentage, and this *interrater reliability* score is used to determine if the data that is being collected is as accurate and reliable as possible.

The program supervisor will frequently review the data taken by the therapists, will probably conduct occasional interrater reliability tests, and will observe programs as they are performed, all to get as full a picture of your child's success as possible.

2. What do the data collection abbreviations mean?

Data collection varies from agency to agency. Your agency will give you information regarding their specific methods of recording data. Table 6.1 shows some commonly used notations that you may see used with your child's program.

Table 6.1 Notations used for recording data

Notation	Stands For	Meaning
PP	Partial Prompt or Physical Prompt	This type of prompt is used when the therapist needs to assist the child, but does not need to motor them through the task.
FP	Full Prompt or Full Physical Prompt	Similar to a hand-over-hand prompt, used when the therapist must motor the child through a task, and the child is not contributing.
HOH	Hand-Over-Hand Prompt	Used when the therapist must motor the child completely through a task, and the child is not contributing.

NR	No Response	Child does not respond in any way.
I	Independent or Incorrect	Child responds correctly without any prompting. Some programs use I to indicate an incorrect response.
C +	Correct	Child responded correctly, without any prompting.
GP	Gesture Prompt	The therapist used a gesture, such as pointing, to prompt. Some agencies may consider eye contact, such as the therapist glancing at the correct choice, as a gesture prompt.
MP	Model Prompt	The therapist performs the task prior to the child performing it themselves.
MP	Material Prompt	See "Positional Prompt" (PS).
SC	Self-Correction	The child, after initially incorrectly responding, has corrected him/herself without any assistance. Some agencies may record this as a +SC, or as a -SC, depending on if they view a self-correction as correct or incorrect.
M	Mastered	A skill that has been learned and generalized to different settings.
RR	Random Rotation	Trials of a variety of knowledge in the same skill set. For example, a therapist may randomly rotate photos of animals, asking "What animal?", for a variety of animal species.

Table continues

Table 6.1 Notations used for recording data *cont.*

Notation	Stands For	Meaning
PS	Positional Prompt	The therapist uses this kind of prompt to indicate that he may have positioned materials to give the child a greater chance of success.
-	Minus or Incorrect	Incorrect response.
Sd	Discriminative Stimulus	The instruction given to the child. If the student were given a matching task, then the Sd in this case would be the word "Match." A Sd gives the child an opportunity to: • respond correctly • respond incorrectly • show no response.
R+	Reinforcement, Reinforcer	The toy or activity that the child is motivated by.
P/PT	Probe/Pre-Test	A pre-test that gives the therapist insight into the student's skills and areas of knowledge.

3. How can I begin to collect data myself?

Since parent involvement in their child's ABA education is so important, most ABA agencies encourage active parent participation in all aspects of the session. One of the best ways to include parents is to teach them to run programs themselves and to take accurate data. In the beginning, the therapist or supervisor may ask that the parent quietly observe so that they may get a feel for what happens during the session. Next, they may be asked to observe the therapist working on programs, and to take simple data that specifies only if a task was done correctly or incorrectly. Later, the therapist will teach the parent how to determine the level of prompting required, how to calculate the percentage correct, and finally, if the program may be moved forward.

For each program, there are specific instructions and prompts given. For a child who may have 20 or more programs, that means that you will be learning all 20 of them. But don't feel overwhelmed. Although the nature of each program is different, the data collection is essentially the same. If you are interested in learning to take data and run programs, and your child's program doesn't already include this, ask the supervisor to be sure the therapist sets aside time to teach you how to do it. Eventually, you will feel comfortable running a complete session by yourself, and thus can continue your child's education during vacations or times when the therapist may be ill.

4. What is "mastery"?

Each ABA agency has specific requirements that deal with mastery of skills. In its most simple terms, mastery means whether or not a program has been learned to fluency. Remember the first few times you got gas when you learned to drive? I do. The first time, I felt pretty unsure of myself. I wasn't really even sure if I was putting in diesel or unleaded gas. I definitely did not show mastery of pumping gas! But as time went by, I became more and more comfortable with the task. I found that I was pumping gas without even really thinking about it! I was pretty fluent in the job of selecting gas, paying for it, and the act of getting it from the pump to my car. When I was able to do it effortlessly, without error, and without having to concentrate on it, I had mastered the task of pumping gas.

Mastery for an ABA program is very similar. We want to see that a child has learned the task, and can show us that he has learned it, quickly, and without error, at least three consecutive times. An additional requirement is that this success be shown with more than one instructor, and at least two instructors, across three different days, to show mastery. Once you become more adept at reading data, you will begin to quickly identify what programs are mastered, and when it happened.

5. What is the significance of 80–90 percent mastery?

Expanding on Question 4, mastery needs to be shown at 80–90 percent, across at least two instructors, across three different days. That 80–90 percent means that your child must obtain a score of at least 80 percent to potentially be considered as moving forward with the program.

6. Are there different ways to collect data? What are they?

There are a variety of ways in which data can be collected:

- A-B-C data collection (see Question 1, p.78)

- scatterplot (a data measurement technique that shows patterns in problem behavior and how it relates to different periods of time)

- time-sampling (a measurement of behavior in specific time intervals, such as every 15 minutes)

- permanent products (can be used when the behavior creates a lasting product—examples of permanent products are number of math problems completed or items thrown during a tantrum).

7. What is a "trend," in regards to data?

A trend, in regards to data, is the general direction taken by a data path. Trends can show an increase, decrease, or no change in behavior. Look at the graphs in Figure 6.1:

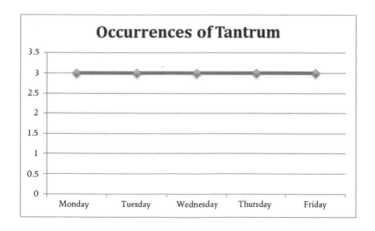

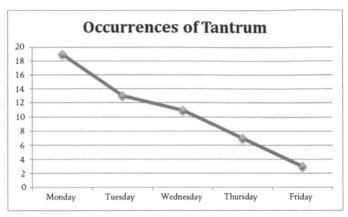

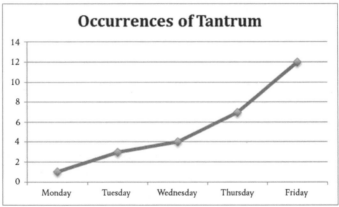

FIGURE 6.1 EXAMPLES OF TRENDS IN DATA

Easy, right? The first graph shows no trend, that is, the behavior has stayed at a steady rate for the whole week. The second graph shows a decreasing trend, and the final graph shows an increasing trend in the behavior.

8. What is "baseline"?

Data gathered prior to implementation of an intervention program is called baseline data. It is what is happening NOW, before the ABA team has begun teaching a new behavior or working to change an existing behavior. In many cases, baseline data can be taken and serves as a point of comparison for learned skills in the future. If three-year-old Pat cannot name any animals when they are shown to him on photo cards, his baseline data will indicate this. Pat's therapists will implement a program that teaches Pat to name common farm animals, and will take detailed data on his progress. This new data can be compared against Pat's baseline and will give a clearer picture of his learning.

Sometimes, it is not in a child's best interest to take baseline data. If a child is exhibiting extremely dangerous behaviors, such as running into traffic, the ABA team should immediately begin their intervention without counting the number of times the child attempts to run into the street. Baseline data should only be taken if it is safe and appropriate to do so.

PART 3

Getting More Involved and Looking to the Future

CHAPTER 7

What's Next?

Vignette: Mr. and Mrs. Adams

Kay and Doug Adams have two-year-old twin boys, Kevin and Kyle. The boys were born premature, and Kay left her job as a California state sheriff's department dispatcher to care for them. Doug is a physician and works long hours in the local hospital's emergency department. He frequently leaves home early and returns late, and spends most of his time with his family on his days off, Monday and Tuesday.

When the boys were 18 months old, Kay noticed that Kyle's eye contact seemed to decrease, and within one month, Kyle was making almost no eye contact at all. He also began engaging in stereotyped behaviors, like hand flapping and spinning in circles. Kyle's doctor referred him to a state agency, which referred Kyle to a psychiatrist who gave Kyle a provisional diagnosis of autism. The California Regional Center set up an in-home ABA program. The ABA therapists come three times a week for two hours each time, and work with Kyle on his goals, as well as incorporating playtime with Kevin and Kay.

Even though Kay is happy that Kyle is receiving services for his autism, she has felt increasingly lonely and depressed. Her only contact with other adults during the week is with the ABA therapists. Her isolation is compounded by her unwillingness to take the boys to the park by herself, since she feels that other parents won't understand her son's differences. In fact, Kay has not been back to the neighborhood park since she noticed other children staring when Kyle tried to spin in circles.

Kay's situation is not unusual. Many parents of children with special needs can find themselves feeling isolated and without support. Children with autism or other disabilities may behave differently than other children in environments such as the grocery store, or on the playground. It can be intimidating to meet other parents if you worry that they will not understand your child's diagnosis, or if you worry that they will judge you for your child's behavior.

Children with autism may also receive other services such as occupational therapy, physical therapy, or speech therapy. The responsibility of driving their children to services may fall on the parent who stays at home, or who can more easily adapt their schedule to accommodate the child's needs. For this reason, it's important that parents remember to expand their opportunities for socializing with other parents, especially parents of children with special needs.

1. Where can I meet other people who have kids with autism?

There are lots of ways to meet families who are dealing with similar issues. Some ABA agencies sponsor a monthly playgroup, where all families of children being served by the agency meet to socialize, support each other, and let their children practice social skills. You might be surprised to learn that a family with a child the same age as yours is being served by the same agency, and lives just around the corner.

ABA agencies also sometimes offer a "family date night," where they will provide respite services (babysitting). This gives parents and guardians valuable time to themselves, without the worries of leaving their child with a babysitter who may not understand the special needs of their child. If your ABA agency doesn't offer these types of services, let them know you are interested! You are not the only parent who needs support, so let them know as well that you are anxious to meet other families like yours.

You may also find other local support groups or playgroups through the local chapter of the Autism Society (www.autism-society.org). The Autism Society provides a wealth of information for individuals with autism and their families, as well as for professionals and teachers.

There are several online support groups, and you may be able to find a group that meets in your area by a simple online search. Check with your child's doctor as well, as there may be a support group or playgroup sponsored by your medical insurance company. See Appendix 1 for more resources.

2. How do I know how my child compares to other kids on the spectrum?

Parents always want to know how their child compares to other children. It's natural to be curious about how well your child is doing, or how they compare to other children their age who also have autism. But it's very, very important to remember that children with autism truly fall somewhere on the spectrum of ability. Imagine a spectrum of color, from red to orange, green to blue, to dark purple. No one color is more beautiful or more meaningful than another color, and each color has unique traits and beauty. Always keep in mind that you have the most perfect child for YOU…your child is in your life because you are equipped to teach them, advocate for them, and raise them to be the most capable adult possible. No matter where they fall on the spectrum, you will see that their talents are unique and unmatched.

3. My friend's daughter has autism. She is already talking and my son isn't. What's wrong?

See Question 2. Your child is unique, and through lots of hard work, they will reach their maximum potential. Comparing two children with autism is like comparing apples to oranges. They are similar, but there is just no way to really relate the two. As you network with other families, you will surely meet children who are talking more, talking less, making eye contact, making NO eye contact, and on and on. Focus on your child and their abilities, and you will feel less of the need to compare them to other children.

4. What if I want more training in ABA?

Sometimes, life brings you to places that you never expected to go. You may never have heard the term "autism" until a doctor told you that your child had autism. You have emerged from a whirlwind of emotions and learning that has brought you to this place, where you are now an expert advocate for your child and have a level of empathy for other families confronted with autism that even the most experienced professionals may not have. If you want to go further in your learning about ABA and how skills in ABA can help your family and others, investigate how a certificate or degree in ABA can help.

The Behavior Analyst Certification Board (BACB®) provides a comprehensive list of approved university training in ABA. You can find that list at www.bacb.com/index.php?page=100358. The Association for Behavior Analysis International (ABAI) also provides useful information on ABA, training, and research. See Appendix 1 for contact details, and for other resources.

5. How can I make my own picture schedule or communication boards myself?

Your in-home ABA provider should include these materials as part of your child's program. If you want quicker access to these materials, you can make your own by searching online for the actual product or activity, downloading a picture, and printing it out. Remember to always observe copyright laws and only use photos that are copyright free or have an open copyright. You can also use commercial photo/icon software or an online-based program. See:

- Boardmaker: www.mayer-johnson.com

- Mrs. Riley: www.mrsriley.com.

6. I read about autism online all the time, and there seems to be so many new therapies to try. Which ones should I try? Which ones should I avoid?

Fortunately, autism resources are just a click away on the computer. You can search the word "autism" and find thousands of resources for treatments, diet, schools, and medication. Wading through the tide of autism information is a mighty task. Remember, though, that for every newfangled autism treatment that proponents report works, there is another that has not worked, or even caused serious harm to a child. Remember some important tips when researching treatments and methodologies:

- Research, research, research! Look carefully at peer-reviewed studies that are funded by a non-involved source. Make note of the year the study was conducted, the number of participants in the study, and the purported results.

- Don't rely 100 percent on anecdotal evidence! Anecdotal evidence is just that: anecdotal. Suggestions from friends or other parents of children with autism are not equivalent to well-conducted research. Use a scientific, medical perspective when evaluating claims about autism treatments.

- Science, science, science! Having a child with autism places you into a land you never dreamed you'd travel. Claims of drastic improvement in behavior and abilities MUST be scientifically validated. If they are not, stay away.

7. Where can I get information about ABA studies that have already been done?

First of all, congratulate yourself on taking the initiative to learn more. You can find many studies about ABA online, especially at the *Journal of Applied Behavior Analysis*. Simply search their name online. A local college or university will have access to journal articles and books on ABA. If you are an alumnus or a student, your university may already give you unlimited access to journal articles when you search for them through the university's library online. Ask your program supervisor for journal articles about specific topics or if you are having difficulty finding adequate information.

8. What progress can I expect my child to make as he grows older?

All children develop differently, and children with special needs are no exception. The clever thing about ABA programs is that although each skill, when viewed alone, may not seem to be leading to anything, for each targeted skill, there is a path that led to the skill, and definite skills that lead away from it. A good example is task completion skills such as building with blocks. Imagine a two-and-a-half-year-old boy who is building a tower of four blocks. Viewed alone, this tower of four blocks may not look like much. But when you go back and see where it began, you will see that this boy would not even stack one block on top of another when his in-home program began. Now, he sits at the table, works for several minutes, plays at the table when he is finished with a task, and enjoys session time and working with his therapist. After he masters a tower of eight blocks, he may learn to build specific models. At first, he may be given blocks that are identical to the therapist's, and be asked to copy a simple four-block structure. Eventually, he may be shown a picture of an advanced ten-block structure, given 20 blocks of varying sizes and colors, and asked to build the structure after the picture is removed. The imitation, problem solving, and social skills he is developing are ones that will be used throughout his lifetime. Your child's skills and abilities are unique, but you can expect that if you maintain the ABA approach, you will clearly be able to see where you are going, and where you came from.

9. How long do ABA programs usually continue for?

The length of an ABA program varies depending on the needs of your child, whether or not they are benefitting from the program, whether or not the program is appropriate for them, and of course, if funding for the program continues to be available. In some states, in-home programs are prohibited from focusing on academic goals, as the general understanding is that the local school district will take over that portion of the child's education.

10. What might be the next step after an ABA program?

You should always be looking forward at what is next for your child. When your child is receiving an in-home treatment program, you should already be looking forward to the next step, whether that is preschool, kindergarten, elementary school, and so on. Frequent evaluation of goals and expected outcomes is imperative if the goals you have chosen for your child (or they have chosen for themselves, in some cases), are to become reality. Your interest in, research of, and involvement in all aspects of your child's education will help them reach their maximum potential.

Resources for Families

United States

Association for Science in Autism Treatment
www.asatonline.org

Autism Research Foundation
www.theautismresearchfoundation.com

Autism Society of America
www.autism-society.org

Autism Speaks
www.autismspeaks.org

Doug Flutie, Jr. Foundation for Autism
www.dougflutiejrfoundation.org

National Foundation for Autism Research
www.nfar.org

Kids Included Together (KIT)
www.kitonline.org

National Inclusion Project
www.inclusionproject.org

The Hollyrod Foundation
www.hollyrod.org

Wrightslaw Special Education Law and Advocacy
www.wrightslaw.org

Association for Behavior Analysis International
www.abainternational.org

Behavior Analyst Certification Board
www.bacb.com

Canada

Autism Speaks
www.autismspeaks.ca

Autism Society Canada
www.autismsocietycanada.ca

Autism Spectrum Disorders Canadian-American Research Consortium
www.asdcarc.com

Canadian Autism Intervention Research Network
www.cairn-site.com

Ministry of Children and Youth Services
www.children.gov.on.ca/mcys

Canadian Autism Spectrum Disorders Alliance
www.asdalliance.org

The Canadian National Autism Foundation
www.cnaf.net

United Kingdom

The National Autistic Society
www.autism.org.uk

UK Autism Foundation
www.ukautismfoundation.org

Autism UK Independent
www.autismuk.com

Autism Centre for Education and Research
www.birmingham.ac.uk/research/activity/education/acer/index.aspx

Centre for Research for Autism and Education
www.ioe.ac.uk/research/28033.html

Research Autism
www.researchautism.net

Australia

Australian Advisory Board on Autism Spectrum Disorders
www.autismadvisoryboard.org.au

Autism Partnership Australia
www.autismpartnership.com.au

Autism Aspergers Advocacy Australia
www.a4.org.au/a4

Autism Awareness
www.autismawareness.com.au

Australian Government Department of Education, Employment, and Workplace Relations
www.deewr.gov.au

Autism SA
www.autismsa.org.au

Autism Asperger ACT
www.autismaspergeract.com.au

List of Reinforcing Phrases

- Good job!
- Awesome!
- Super!
- Fantastic!
- You're doing great!
- Wow!
- Yay!
- Amazing!

- Superstar!
- Incredible!
- High-five!
- Bravo!
- Hurray!
- You tried so hard!
- Good try!
- You've got it!

Bibliography

Centers for Disease Control and Prevention (2012) "Autism spectrum disorders: Data and statistics." Available at www.cdc.gov/ncbddd/autism/data.html, accessed on 17 September 2012.

Cipani, E. and Schock, K. (2010) *Functional Behavioral Assessment, Diagnosis, and Treatment: A Complete System for Education and Mental Health Settings (Second Edition)*. New York, NY: Springer Publishing.

Cooper, J.O., Heron, T.E., and Heward, W.L. (2007) *Applied Behavior Analysis (Second Edition)*. Upper Saddle River, NJ: Pearson.

Green, G., Maurice, C., and Luce, S. (eds) (1996) *Behavioral Intervention for Young Children With Autism: A Manual for Parents and Professionals (First Edition)*. Austin, TX: Pro-Ed.

Kearney, A.J. (2008) *Understanding Applied Behavior Analysis: An Introduction to ABA for Parents, Teachers, and Other Professionals (First Edition)*. London, England: Jessica Kingsley Publishers.

Offit, P.A. (2008) *Autism's False Prophets: Bad Science, Risky Medicine, and the Search for a Cure*. New York, NY: Columbia University Press.

Index